The Artist Must Be Fed

The Broke Artists' Cookbook and Guide to Entertaining on the Cheap

by Les Sterling

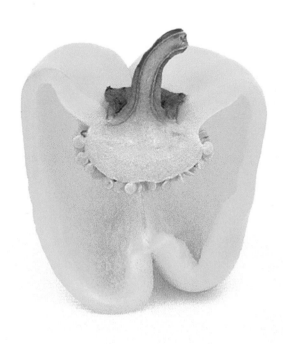

For Bree
who asked me to write this book 25 years ago

When I became an adult, some time around 1993, I already knew how to cook - sort of. My mother, in her wisdom, taught me the basics - how to brown onions, how to make a pie crust, how to shop for groceries on a shoestring budget, and how to make those groceries last. But, I realized at some point in my early adulthood that I was in a strange little minority. Very few of my fellow Gen-X twentysomething friends knew how to navigate the kitchens of their first apartments. Many stocked up on canned soup, and macaroni and cheese - but would forget to buy butter and milk. In 1993, I was by no means an expert in the kitchen, but I realized I had been given a gift that would make it possible for my broke-ass artist self to eat cheaply, and more importantly, to eat relatively well.

Amongst my cadre of friends, we each had some sort of skill or access to supplies. My friend Sara and I could cook, many of us worked in restaurants, a couple of folks delivered pizza, a few worked in retail, and a couple folks worked in grocery stores. The thing we all had in common? We were all broke-ass artists. Most of us in school full-time, also working full-time, trying to make ends meet while living hand to mouth. At some point, we realized that by combining our powers and access, none of us would have to ever go hungry. The friends with grocery store jobs would help make sure our totals at the register were, shall we say, "minimized," and they would frequently come home with bags of produce and packaged foods that were destined for disposal due to their nearing expiration. That's when we learned how to swiftly prep something and freeze it, pickle it or just cook a lot of something and share it. This is where the cooking and canning skills that my mother had the forethought to bestow on me would come in handy. Naturally, a lot of refining of these skills was essential. Many evenings were spent in dumpster dives and trips to thrift stores looking for kitchen tools, useful pots, pans, and canning jars - more than plentiful on thrift store shelves at the time. In the 90's, the canning of food had fallen out of common practice and fashion, and it would be another 15 years before hipsters would discover the ironic use of canning jars as cocktail glasses - a practice that, for the record, really never lost favor among the broke classes.

In this book, there are going to be recipes, of course, some discussion of techniques, and some general advice about what to do in your kitchen - plus a lot of my commentary and rambling. As much as possible, in this volume, I try to give you recipes that aren't terribly difficult, that don't require a bunch of expensive ingredients and don't need expert level techniques. Some are a little more advanced, of course, but I try my best to make the instructions as clear as possible – fancy looking food is sometimes easier than you think. And sometimes, you want a little fancy in your life, and once you master a few simple techniques, low-key fancy is always within your grasp.

It's at this point in this prologue that I should explain something: I'm not a professional chef, or even a professional cook. In my twenties I worked in some restaurant kitchens and hated working in that environment. One might say that I was "temperamentally unsuited" to that work - meaning that I was the worst possible personality type for a professional kitchen - I was the curious, thinky, creative, intellectual type… hell, I still am. Unfortunately, that's a personality trait that I am incapable of turning off. Restaurant cooking is absolutely nothing like cooking at home. It was no fun for me – professional kitchens aren't a place to improvise or explore, and that's all I wanted to do. I wanted to know why you "monter au beurre" and at what point you do that. I wanted to see demi glace being made and to know how to do it best, and how to change it up. These are things I could have learned at culinary school, but I was going to art school to learn how to be a photographer, and I had no interest in spending tens of thousands of dollars to learn to make stock. Restaurants, out of necessity, need people to do as they're told, and to be able to repeat the same recipe over and over again, with zero deviation from the formula. THAT is just not my thing.

However, in my time working in restaurants, both in the kitchen and in Front of House positions as waiter, bartender and manager, I learned some pro techniques and I've learned to adapt them to my "real life" kitchen, not as a chef, but as an artist and writer. And since I've spent my life and career as an artist and writer, I've spent most of that time figuring out how to make a budget go as far as possible while still being able to make things delicious. Sometimes, you have to make do with what you have, or what you can access. There's no reason that it can't also be delicious.

Most importantly, right now, I'm going to divulge the biggest secret to extraordinary culinary success.
Ready for it?
Here's the secret: *There isn't one.*

There isn't a singular tool, skill or ingredient that, in an instant, will transform your food to the level of a three Michelin star restaurant. Like every other skill, practice is the only way to get there. Annoying, I know. But most "failures" in the kitchen usually aren't complete "failures." Your first attempt at vegan lasagna might be a terrifying and squishy abomination in your eyes - **but** I bet it's tasty! Okay, if it's burnt, maybe that's one that you throw away and start over. But remember, there's a lesson in there - perhaps about oven temperature or baking time? Maybe it needs more moisture?

If there's one underlying lesson that I can convey throughout, it's that technique is really more important than access to expensive ingredients or tools. Spending a ton of money on your ingredients won't magically make your food amazing - truly, there's nothing sadder than seeing a $75 beef rib destroyed by ineptitude at the oven.

Now, that isn't to say that better ingredients won't help - but better doesn't equate to expensive. Remember, your major chain grocery stores are SO much more expensive than they need to be – you aren't paying for better stuff at the supermarket, you're just paying for the convenience of having everything in one place. Look for a store that specializes in produce. Look for a spice market. Look for a butcher. You might be surprised how much money you'll save just by going to a produce market to buy your fruit and vegetables. Bulk bins sometimes offer excellent savings over a pre-packaged version, but not always. Sometimes, it's been sitting there a while. Smell everything. If it smells weird, obviously, don't buy it. In the case of the bulk bins, frequently, something that's old or off is obvious by the fragrance.

Remember, too, that it's okay to be skeptical of what you're seeing while you're out shopping. Just because something is calling itself Organic, or Cage-Free, or Grass Fed doesn't always mean what you think or hope that it does. Sadly, The United States does a pretty poor job of regulating the way in which food products are made and marketed, so the language being used on labels doesn't necessarily mean anything. This, of course, is ever evolving. But as of 2020, food regulations work to serve the interests of mass corporate agricultural entities - not your dinner table and not your health. Also be skeptical of All-Natural or Natural - those terms truly mean nothing. I'm not saying to not buy them, just be aware product marketing is a multi-billion dollar industry, and the creation of the actual product receives less time and attention than the marketing of that product will receive. Read the ingredient lists, and learn what the weird words mean. Not all the "science-y" sounding words are bad.

A quick note on how to use this book: For better or worse, I've been told that my recipes don't really read like traditional recipes. I editorialize a LOT. I comment and frequently over-explain. I provide alternatives and modifications and try as best I can to describe what you should be seeing and smelling. As with any recipe you ever use - read the whole thing first before you get into it, make sure you have everything you'll need.

When you're cooking, remember that you have some space to improvise. Take some chances - substitute herbs you like more once you get a sense of what goes well together, add more chili powder when you want more burning spice heat. Experimentation is how you grow.

When it comes to baking, however, I'd recommend sticking to the recipe the first couple times before you try to riff. Remember: Baking is Science. Cooking is Art.

If you already have some basic knowledge of how to cook, these recipes will be effortless. But if you are truly new to your kitchen, if you are one of those folks that only uses your kitchen to store your coffee maker and microwave, I'm confident that these will still be manageable recipes that you can prepare without (much) injury or trauma.

Hopefully this book will make it easier, save you some money and maybe even make you laugh.

Enjoy!

TABLE OF CONTENTS

Let's talk about stocking your kitchen. Before we get into this, perhaps take a quick inventory of what you already have in your cabinets and refrigerator. While you're doing that, take a look at the expiration dates. Are they currently past that expiration date? Go check. I'll wait...

SIDEBAR ON EXPIRATION DATES: *There are definitely things that you can keep past their expiration dates – don't get me wrong – but there are some things that really should be thrown out. Honestly, it isn't even necessarily that they've gone "bad," it's just that the flavors and/or efficacy will be compromised. Expired baking powder? Useless. Throw it out. Pickles in your refrigerator a month past expiry? Meh, they're probably fine, but taste them. If they're starting to taste like metal, throw them away. It won't necessarily HURT you to keep eating them, but they're going to stop being quite as tasty.*
And, of course, if something has actual mold or discoloration on it, throw it away.

There are three major areas to plan for when you're putting your kitchen together:

Your Pantry – these are items to keep in a cool (less than about 72 degrees Fahrenheit), dry place. Heat and humidity are the enemy of things like spices, sugar and flour, as well as oils and vinegar. Cool and dry are imperative.

Your Freezer – you know that part of your refrigerator where you store your vodka and ice cubes? Yeah, you can keep many kinds of vegetables in there for up to a year.

Your Refrigerator – In spite of what you might have been told, your condiments don't last forever. Start looking at expiration dates.

In an effort to keep things as simple and economical as possible, I'm going to give you a list of the essentials. Anything you have beyond the list is a nice perk, but please don't feel like you need a bottle of 20-year, barrel aged balsamic vinegar to survive day to day – your salads will be fine. Always keep in mind that how much you'll need of something depends entirely on how fast you're going to use it.

PRO TIP: *You probably won't need a 20 pound sack of flour if you aren't baking very much. While buying massive amounts of something CAN make things more affordable, ounce for ounce, those savings aren't real if you throw out a bunch because it becomes too old to use. If you're going to the wholesale club for "economy" size bags of flour, sugar, etc. consider going in with a few friends and share the bounty. Ounce for ounce, it's considerably cheaper. Everybody wins.*

- CHAPTER 1 -

Planning Your Pantry

For those who aren't necessarily at-home culinary enthusiasts, the pantry is the area that seems to suffer most. Maybe you have some salt, and a half a bag of sugar, but what do you have for spices? Are you keeping and using dried herbs in a way that releases their potential? Or are you holding them hostage in hopes that one day you'll really need that dried rosemary? Remember, these all want to be stored in a relatively cool, dry location. And even in ideal conditions, they do lose their flavor eventually.

While this is not, by any means, an exhaustive or complete list of what you might find useful to have in the pantry, this is a good start.

PRO TIP: *Keep a permanent marker in your kitchen tool drawer to write the dates you open the package. The clock really starts on something going bad when you OPEN it, not the "Best by" date.*

THE ESSENTIALS

Baking Powder – If you're making cakes, biscuits or non-yeast breads, it's an essential to have around. If not, you might be able to live without it. Definitely pay attention to the date on the container. It doesn't spoil, as such, but it will lose its efficacy as it ages, and will lose its ability to leaven your biscuits.

Baking Soda – Different from Baking POWDER, Baking soda has uses beyond just baking. It's an excellent cleaning product, and the best way to keep odors from getting crazy in your refrigerator. Leave an opened box in the fridge, and change it out after 6 months. The one in your cabinet should be usable and effective for a year.

Brown Sugar – Imperative if you're a baker or love baked beans. But generally, a one-pound box or bag is plenty for most needs. No matter what climate you live in, it will clump up. But you can include a marshmallow, or clean shard of terra cotta in the package to keep things from clumping too firmly. Light brown is probably the most universally useful variety, but dark brown has a much richer flavor.

Canned Tomatoes – This is one of the few canned things that I'll advocate for over keeping fresh. Fresh tomatoes are great, of course. But they'll only last for a week or so before they become overripe and decay. Canned will keep for years, and through some alchemical magic, canned tomatoes don't really lose their nutritional value. I'm not a nutritionist, that's for sure, but I believe the science. I do know that the flavor is more concentrated, and you can get away with using less canned than fresh when you're making sauces. You'll find canned whole tomatoes, chopped/diced, crushed, and some that include green chilis, some that have olive oil and herbs, and any number of other varieties. For basic planning, I'd suggest having a couple larger (24-28 oz) cans of crushed tomatoes, and a couple of the diced kind.

Tomato Paste – Remember, tomato paste is NOT the same as tomato sauce. Tomato paste is thickened tomato puree. Cans of tomato paste tend to be relatively inexpensive, and are super useful to add to tomato sauce that's very watery to help thicken it up. Always a good idea to have a couple cans in the cabinet. You can also find tomato paste in tubes for smaller applications - a spoonful in soup to add umami and richness is marvelous! The tube version of tomato paste tends to be more expensive, but the convenience of being able to dispense small amounts is sometimes worth it.

Other Canned Vegetables – Canned beans are always a good idea to have on hand - you can cook and rehydrate dry beans, of course, but canned beans are a much quicker solution when time is a factor. Kidney Beans are good for chili and salads. If you like hummus, keep a couple cans of chickpeas around for an easy version you can make at home (that recipe's in here, too). But other canned vegetables? Meh. There's the occasional recipe that'll pop up that needs a can of creamed corn or something, but for the most part, save that money and buy frozen or fresh. I mean, canned asparagus? No, thank you. Some things are truly best when they're fresh.

Cooking Oil – This one can be a bit tricky in the grocery store. There are SO many on the shelf, so if you're unfamiliar with all the differences, it can all blend together and become overwhelming.

For most purposes, I recommend that you just look for the simplest option - and usually the least expensive. Either Canola Oil, or one that just calls itself "Vegetable Oil" is perfectly fine for most uses. Ideally, you're looking for something that can be suitable for frying, baking and for salad dressings, so something neutral in flavor is best. Corn oil and Peanut Oils are great, but are much better for frying, okay for baking but not great as salad dressings, because they bring so much of their own flavor.

A major factor to consider in cooking oils is what is called "Smoke Point" – that is, the temperature at which the oil starts to smoke, break down, burn, and no longer be edible. For instance, Sesame, Walnut and Almond Oils and most nut and seed oils are great for marinades, sauces, etc, but shouldn't ever be heated much. Extra Virgin Olive Oils are great for cold salad dressings, but can also be used for sautes, where the cooking temperature will be around 275-300 degrees Fahrenheit. But for deep frying, where the temperature needs to be at least 350 degrees, you'll want to look to vegetable oils like Canola, Corn, Sunflower, Grapeseed or Safflower oils that can get into the higher range without breaking down.

Any cooking oil will start to go rancid after several months, especially if it's exposed to heat or excessive humidity. If you have an open bottle of oil for more than a few months, just give it a sniff. Rancid oil puts off a scent that is unmistakable. You won't wonder if it's gone off - it will absolutely let you know.

Corn Starch – Generally sold in a 12-16 oz box, or plastic container. Any brand is fine. Cornstarch doesn't really ever spoil but be careful not to cross contaminate because introducing moisture or other elements can cause mold to develop.

Flour – All-purpose (or, AP) unbleached white flour. Usually sold in 4-5 pound bags, but also frequently available in a smaller 2 lb type for those who don't bake, or use it very much. If you have enough counter or storage space to put flour into a nice decorative jar or canister, that's a perfectly nice place to store it, provided the jars are airtight. If there's no plastic or rubber gasket seal on the lids, don't bother. You can also store flour very nicely in it's own paper bag, stored inside of a gallon freezer zip closure bag for up to six months. There's also something called "Wondra" - it's essentially an ultra fine flour, specially mixed for use in gravy and sauces, etc. It's nice to have it if you plan on making sauces a lot, but is definitely not essential.

Lentils/Dry Beans – Useful, cheap and you can store them forever. Only get the ones you like - don't get them because you think you need them.

Onions – White or yellow onions are the base of pretty much every dish I make. You probably have a friend who talks about hating onions, but you can just sit back and know that most savory dishes start with some member of genus allium, and they've been eating them without knowing for years. Store them in a cool, dry place and they'll last for weeks. Also, consider shallots. They're more expensive than your everyday onion, but still pretty affordable. They bring a warmer, milder flavor to your dishes, and are far less acrid when eaten raw.

> **SIDEBAR:** A "nice to have" version is dried onion flakes – excellent for marinades, salad dressings and some meat preparations. They tend to have a warm, "toasty" flavor that lends some umami to the dish. They're in amongst the spices at pretty much every store.

Pasta (Dry) – Have a package of spaghetti, one of linguine, a rigatoni or penne, and a fusilli on hand for quick dinners. You'll want macaroni for the Baked Mac & Cheese recipe in this book. Dry pasta is cheap, and has a lot of uses.

Potatoes – Your everyday plain potatoes are a staple and will keep for a month or so if they're kept cool and dry. Once they start to grow "eyes" or roots, you can still dig those out of the potato and they're still edible. Once the roots really get to be a few inches long, then throw those out. Explore the waxier red potatoes or the French Fingerling varieties. They tend to be a little more expensive, but nice for an occasional treat.

Quinoa – In spite of what every poorly conceived, hipster food blog insists, quinoa is not an essential. What it is, though, is delicious, loaded with fiber, and when coupled with legumes can create a complete protein. It also finds itself lower on the glycemic index than many other grains. Prepare it similar to rice.

Rice, White and/or Brown Long-Grain – Cheap, and has a million uses. Look at Jasmine Rice and Basmati as well, for lower starch varieties that aren't as sticky as others.

> **SIDEBAR:** *Rice is truly one of the most diverse grain crops on the planet. Try them all at some point. But you don't need them all in your house all at once.*

Salt – For cooking purposes, I'm partial to kosher salt. But, a cylindrical container of Iodized Table Salt is perfectly fine for most purposes. Store brand is fine – no need to overpay for something this basic. Salt you can keep pretty much forever. It doesn't really go bad but will start to discolor and pick up the flavors of stuff around it if it isn't kept in cool, dry conditions. Kosher salt isn't really any different, other than its larger grains, but I prefer it so I'm able to control the measure of salt going into what I'm making. The conversion between types of salt isn't necessarily 1:1. A teaspoon of kosher salt brings as much salinity as about a half teaspoon of table salt.

Stocks – Beef, Chicken and/or Vegetable. We'll talk about making your own stock later in this book, but as a shortcut, it's nice to have a few options in the cabinet. Buy the ones in the cartons, not in the cans. Also, remember that if something is calling itself "Broth" it will usually be more diluted than "Stock", but still useful for making quick soups and such. Always get the low-sodium variety so you can control how much salt is going into your dish. Don't buy those salty little cubes that you add to water to make broth. The amount of sodium you consume isn't worth the paltry amount of flavor that you're getting out of them.

Sugar – Plain white granulated sugar, sold usually in 4-5 pound bags. Ideal storage conditions are the same as flour, but if you live in a more humid climate, you may find that your sugar will clump together. Nothing wrong with it, just break it apart before you measure. Don't let the inside of your sugar storage get wet. Keep it dry, and you're good for a very long time.

Vanilla Extract – This will be one of those things that'll cost a little more for the good stuff. You can find a cheaper version at every grocery store, but that stuff is going to be pretty light on flavor. If the inexpensive (less than about $5) store brand is the only kind you have, use twice the amount that the recipe calls for.

Vinegar – There are a lot of different kinds of vinegar out there, but if you only have one in your kitchen, have plain white vinegar. A gallon of the stuff only costs a couple bucks, and it has a million uses – both in your food, and as a cleaning product. Red and White Wine Vinegars are great, champagne vinegar is delicious in salad dressings, apple cider vinegar is wonderful in making cabbage, and balsamic vinegar is so ubiquitous that a salad can barely exist without it. If you can get them all, great! They'll all have a wonderful long life in your cabinet and you'll never regret having them. But if you can only have one? Go with the basic white.

OPTIONAL THINGS THAT ARE NICE TO HAVE
BUT THAT YOU CAN TOTALLY LIVE WITHOUT

Arborio Rice – If you plan to make risotto often (and hopefully you will after trying my recipe in here, because it's super delicious!) then Arborio may become more essential. It's a much starchier type of rice, and isn't as universal as plain white or brown long-grain varieties. It can also substitute for the much-harder-to-find Valencia or Bomba rice that's used in paella. In theory, you can use plain, long-grain rice for risotto, but I wouldn't recommend it. It gets mushy and weird.

Caster Sugar – Sometimes called superfine, or bar sugar. It's the same thing as plain white sugar, it's just been ground until it's very fine. It's great for beverages, because it dissolves so quickly – what with the whole "ultrafine" thing – and is occasionally useful when you're making gelatins when you don't want to spend a bunch of time trying to get sugar to dissolve. If you find yourself in the rare situation where you ONLY have Caster Sugar, but need regular sugar, use ½ to ¾ the amount of what the recipe calls for.

Cocoa Powder – Not to be confused with the drinking variety that you use to make chocolate milk. Really, this is really for the baking enthusiasts. Or, if you like making hot chocolate from scratch. Get the best quality you can get. This is one of those occasions where you really do get what you pay for.

Curry Powder – A marvelous blend of spices that was developed in the 19th Century by the English to emulate the flavors they were getting in India at the time. It's nice to have on hand, because it's easier than having all of the individual spices that go into curry powder. Even if you aren't making that many Indian dishes, you'll still find a jar of curry powder useful in other dishes. Sun Brands Madras Curry Powder is good for most general purposes. Vadouvan (not a brand, but a type of curry powder) is another nice French curry blend – mild, with garlic and cumin-forward notes. If you're new to these flavors, keep it mild when you're shopping for a Curry Powder. You can add extra heat later.

Extracts – Generally, I don't think you need a lot of flavor extracts other than vanilla, even if you really love baking. I will say, an almond extract is nice to have around for some cookie and cheesecake recipes. But the others? Meh. Leave them on the shelf if you don't have a particular need in mind. You probably won't have a lot of need for Lime Extract on a daily basis.

Ginger Root (Fresh) – Ginger tends to be pretty cheap, and most recipes that need it don't need that much of it. Store it like you store potatoes, or chop your leftovers into a jar with vodka, and in a week or so you'll have delicious ginger flavored vodka.

Liquid Smoke – I can hear a million chefs screaming at me for even mentioning the existence of liquid smoke, but it definitely has its place. It's one of those "a little goes a long way" products, so get the smallest you can find - it'll last longer than you can use it up before it expires. But again, don't buy it until you have a specific need in mind. It's not an item you'll need very often, but there aren't many easy substitutes when you do.

Powdered Sugar – Sometimes called Confectioners Sugar, or Icing Sugar, it is NOT interchangeable with regular sugar, because it contains corn starch, or sometimes other anti-clumping agents. It's essential to make icing and butter-cream, as well as in some candy and fudge preparations. But until you're wanting to do that, don't worry about having it in your cabinet.

Shortening – When you have vegetable oil, you won't find yourself needing shortening quite as much. But it's an excellent option when you want to make vegan pie crusts and pastries - you can use it as a substitute for butter in many baking situations. Store it like vegetable oil and it'll keep for a surprisingly long time. Manteca/Lard is essentially non-vegan shortening. Because it's literally pork fat that's been clarified so your apple pie crust doesn't taste like ham.

> **SIDEBAR:** *You will likely also find "Butter Flavored" shortening. These are also great but aren't usually a good option if you're cooking vegan. Look at the ingredients. These tend to have milk solids of some variety to lend it that "butter" flavor. Tasty? Yes. Vegan? No.*

Vermouth – Keeping a bottle of relatively inexpensive (<$10) white and/or red vermouth on hand for de-glazing pans can be very useful. I keep mine in the cabinet, but you can also refrigerate it and it'll keep longer. It adds complexity to soups, and roasted dishes that can't be achieved through many other means. An inexpensive, relatively dry white wine will also do the job, but wine tends to not keep as long as a vermouth. By no means should you buy anything calling itself "Cooking Wine" – it usually has salt, and some other mysterious ingredients that I have yet to fully identify, but I'm pretty sure Disappointment is one of them.

Worcestershire Sauce – This sauce is a delight for beef, lamb and other meaty meat dishes. It's a VERY specific flavor, and it's nearly as hard to replicate as it is to pronounce. Nice to have, and it keeps for ages. Note, though - it usually contains anchovies. Coconut Aminos and Bragg's Amino Acids are good substitutes for a fully vegan version.

Soy Sauce – This is one that I nearly had on the essentials list, but you can probably live without it if you had to. Definitely shop at Asian markets for soy sauce - it's considerably cheaper, and you'll find a variety of soy sauces that you never knew existed. Don't be afraid to ask someone if you're not sure where to begin.

A SPECIAL SECTION DEVOTED TO HERBS & SPICES

- Herbs -

Really when it comes to dried herbs, I avoid most of them. There's very little more useless in a kitchen, for instance, than dried parsley or dried basil. I'm sure you've seen those assortments of bottled dried herbs and spices packaged on a cute rack as a gift, and that temptation is SO STRONG to pick one up, and immediately feel like you're armed with so many options!

Resist that urge. You have no idea how old those herbs are, and how they might taste or smell. And those tiny little plastic jars at the grocery store? Nope. Complete garbage. I keep very few dried herbs around, and they only get to stay for 3 months or so, in airtight containers, before they're sent off to the compost heap.

Now that I've COMPLETELY maligned the dry herb industry, let me say this: Dried herbs **can** be helpful, but pick them up from specialty sellers where you will likely find something a little fresher - at least those will have some flavor to them. You'll be surprised how cheap they are when you buy them in bulk.

In theory, dried herbs are meant to be a more concentrated, preserved version of the herb, so you can keep it exponentially longer than the fresh counterparts. The problem with drying herbs in the case of mass manufactured products, is just that - mass manufacture. They're throwing all kinds of quality together and grinding it down and drying them out, leaving them in a warehouse for unknown amounts of time... and they end up tasting very different to their fresh counterparts. The few I keep in my kitchen are ones that I have for long-cooking processes, so there's plenty of time for the flavor to infuse into what I'm making.

Here are three I like to have in the house:

Bay Leaves – essential for most meat or game preparations. Bay Leaves are one of those few herbs that are actually better dried.

Herbes de Provence – A mix of savory, marjoram, rosemary, thyme and oregano, and sometimes lavender. This one isn't REALLY essential, but it's a nice one to have for chicken and fish preparations, and long cooking stews.

Italian Herb Blend – usually a mix of basil, oregano, marjoram and sometimes rosemary. Useful for so many things, and is fairly inexpensive. It tends to hold it's flavor for longer, so you can keep it in your pantry for longer than you think. Just remember - airtight container, in a cool, dry cabinet.

- Spices -

Consider your spices similarly to how you consider your dried herbs. How old are they? Where are they coming from? Their suppliers might have had them for months and months in some warehouse without temperature or humidity control, or in transit before they make it to your grocery shelves. If you're fortunate enough to live in a city where you can find a market that caters to a Latin American or East or South Asian clientele, your spice options will be far more abundant, far more flavorful, and far more affordable. And if you have Middle Eastern and North African groceries in your city, then you truly have near endless options. Here's a list of what I find is essential to have around:

Black Pepper – If you have a peppermill, fresh ground pepper is so much more flavorful than pre-ground. But if not, ground is totally fine for both cooking and table. Be aware of how finely ground it is. Superfine ground pepper tends to dry faster, and lose its flavor.

Chili Powder – Usually chili powder is a blend of a couple types of dried, pulverized chili peppers, cumin and sometimes oregano. It isn't always exceedingly spicy, but it is a good way to add a kick to your dishes. Double check the spice levels before using. There's a difference between Chili Powder and Ground Chilis!

Chinese Five Spice – A delicious mix of clove, Chinese cinnamon, star anise, Szechuan pepper and fennel seed. You might have to dig for it at the grocery store, and try different brands before you find one you like, but it's seriously good for more than you might think.

Cinnamon – You probably don't have a lot of need for cinnamon sticks, but ground cinnamon will come in handy. In addition to making apple pie and cinnamon toast, it's frequently found in North African, Middle Eastern and South Asian cuisine in non-dessert dishes.

Cumin – An essential for Mexican and Indian dishes. The distinct, warm umami flavor is unmistakable, and can't really be duplicated. You can find Ground Cumin or Cumin Seed. Both are great to have, but the ground variety will be the most used if you're a beginner in the kitchen.

Garlic Powder – Not to be confused with Garlic SALT. If you have garlic powder, and table salt, guess what you can make for yourself?

Ground Ginger – Really, this is more of a "nice to have" if you aren't baking much, but it really elevates your chicken soup game. Yes, there's a recipe in here for that.

Paprika – A smoked Spanish variety is extra fancy and nice, but a regular paprika is great. It offers a mild, warm spice without bringing much heat.

Other Spices – There is a limitless number of possible spices you can have, of course, but as with all ingredients, don't buy it if you don't have a use for it. But for the Nice To Have list: Nutmeg, Allspice, Onion Powder, and Crushed Red Pepper flakes.

- CHAPTER 2 -

Filling Your Freezer

Filling Your Freezer

Your freezer can be your best friend when it comes to stocking up. Most frozen vegetables and meats can stay frozen for up to a full year, depending on how well it's sealed. When you buy meat from the grocery store, the foam tray and plastic wrap is only sufficient to protect it from freezer burn for a few weeks.

However, if you find chicken in its original wrapping at the back of your freezer and it's been there for a couple months, move it into a sealable freezer bag. It'll slow the effects of freezer burn. Now, freezer burn doesn't make your food inedible, necessarily, but it can deeply affect the texture and can cause it to appear less appetizing.

VEGETABLES

Spinach, *chopped or whole leaf*
Peas
Corn
Green Beans
Broccoli Florets
Stir-Fry Mix

Generally, I look for the lower priced items when it comes to frozen vegetables. Believe it or not, the only frozen vegetable I'm inclined to spend slightly more to buy is broccoli. Only because cheaper frozen broccoli tends to be a LOT of stems, and fewer florets. Which is fine when you're chopping it down for soup. But if you're looking to have steamed broccoli with dinner? Spend the extra.

INEXPENSIVE MEATS

Use these within a few months, but they'll be fine for a year, if they're well sealed.

Chicken thighs (Boneless, or bone-in)
Thin cut Chicken Breast (sometimes called "Milanese Style")
Beef Chuck Roast - Sometimes a whole roast, or cut into cubes for stew
Ground Beef
Ground Turkey
Italian Sausage (Links, or ground lump)
Pork Tenderloin (small, 1-2 lb strip loins)

Generally speaking, if you're buying more expensive cuts of meat for fancy dinner purposes, don't freeze it. Buy it within a day or two that you're preparing it, and just keep it in the refrigerator. Expensive steaks, beef loin, etc. tend to have their texture compromised when they're frozen for extended periods of time. And if you're buying it to prepare tomorrow, why bother with all that thawing time after it comes out of the freezer? And fish? Don't buy it frozen, and don't freeze it once you get it home. It's always weird, and the texture becomes either grainy or slimy. No, thank you.

PREPARED MEALS/PIZZAS/SNACK FOODS

Now, in terms of nutritional value, these aren't exactly the best of the best. Most frozen pizzas, snacks, desserts and frozen meals TEND to be higher fat, higher salt & sugar and are, like most convenient foods, not great for you. However, part of being broke and busy frequently means having cheap foods that aren't exactly the healthiest options - only because that's what you can afford. How many times have you been at the grocery store to see single-serve frozen pastas selling for about $1? I am not a nutritionist of any kind, and I'm not going to tell you what you should and should not buy *(I'm kidding, I'm gonna tell you that a lot in this book)*. All I have to say about frozen meals, pizza and that sort of food is "Everything In Moderation".

I mean, frozen mac and cheese is truly delicious. If you feel guilt about having it for dinner, throw some frozen broccoli on it. Delicious!

- CHAPTER 3 -

Readying Your Refrigerator

Refrigerators are a magical thing. It's where the delicious, ready-to-eat and quick-to-make stuff lives. It can also be a terrifying graveyard of decaying left-overs and liquefied salad greens if you don't keep up on it. Of all places in your kitchen, this is where you must pay attention to expirations. I'm always enter-tained by people out shopping with a cart FILLED with glorious fresh vegetables, and I always wonder if they're feeding a bunch of people, or if they're just leav-ing those fabulous veggies to die in the refrigerator. The crisper drawer is where you will find your biggest opportunity to throw money in the trash - by overbuy-ing things you don't need, and then allowing it to turn into compost.

But, condiments do tend to last a while, and are an excellent thing to keep a va-riety of around. After all, more condiments mean more options! But, It would be near impossible for me to make an "Essentials" list for your refrigerator, because so much is subjective. Obviously, you should shop to your tastes. No need to have three kinds of mustard if you don't use them or like them. Same with mayon-naise, or ketchup. Do you like pickles? No? Then don't buy them. The conundrum comes because many of those things can also be ingredients in delicious things that you might want to make later. Salad dressings are essential for fresh greens, of course, but consider that vinaigrettes are also just marinades waiting to realize their full potential. Ketchup and barbeque sauce? Your meatloaf would be bor-ing without them. Mustard and mayonnaise? No one wants dry tuna salad. And french fries can only ever be improved by dipping in most any of those.

Things like fruit juices tend to hang on for a week or more, same with milk. Remember, the "Sell By/Best By" date is the date that markets use to identify the point at which they should remove it from the shelf. It doesn't mean that it's au-tomatically spoiled. But if your milk is a week past the "best by" date, make sure to give it a sniff before you use it. Spoiled milk is pretty unequivocal in letting you know when it's done.

Also, every week or two, clean out your refrigerator. Wipe down each shelf with some sort of bleachy, anti-bacterial cleanser and wipe up all those spills and weird droplets that have come from who knows where. Those spills and spots are a breeding ground for germs, and accelerates decay in your fridge. It's also a good chance to sort through the expired and the dead vegetables.

Remember that how you store food has all to do with where you live. If you live in a hot, humid climate, that will affect how you choose to store root vegetables - potatoes don't like to be too warm, or too moist. They may mistake a dark, warm and humid cabinet for being underground, so they'll start growing roots. But a cooler, drier environment will let them keep longer. If you live in a hot climate, and don't have air conditioning, the cooking oils and condiments on your shelves have a shortened life expectancy.

A few notes on what to keep, or not keep, in the refrigerator:

Apples – Okay, technically you CAN refrigerate apples, but for me, they tend to get mealy and lose their natural sweetness. But if you have them for pies or cooking purposes, that's completely fine. If you put them in the fridge, keep them away from carrots. They hate each other and try to kill each other by making each other rot faster. Why? Um, because... science? Also, sliced apples start browning immediately. Rub them with lemon juice to keep the oxidation under control.

Asparagus – It has always seemed like asparagus was a "USE IT NOW!" vegetable - thinking that it wouldn't possibly survive for long in the fridge. But, it'll keep far longer if you treat it like your fresh herbs or fresh flowers. Cut off the dry, bottom bit of the stem, and put it in a jar with an inch of water, and refrigerate. Your asparagus will keep far longer.

Avocados – Storing avocados next to bananas will only help them both. Sit them next to each other on the counter, or in a paper bag, and the bananas will help the avocado ripen nicely. Once you've sliced open an avocado, though, sprinkle the inside with lemon juice and store it in an airtight container, in the refrigerator. They oxidize and turn brown VERY fast. It doesn't mean they're inedible, just really, really unappealing. And no one wants beige guacamole.

> **SIDEBAR:** *When you buy avocados, look for them to be ALMOST ripe. If they're already ripe, unless you're eating them immediately, they'll be overripe by the time you get around to them. How can you tell if they're ripe? Push gently into the skin on the fattest part of the avocado. If it yields easily, then it's probably ready to go. If it's still firm, it needs a couple days before it's ripe.*

Bread – This truly baffles me. Why, oh why, would you keep bread in the refrigerator? It's inviting bacterial growth, and dries it out. If you're really stocking up on bread, and have too much to use before it goes bad, then throw it in the freezer. It'll never again be as good as fresh, but after it thaws, it'll still be reasonably tasty. But in the fridge? You're just making it inedible.

Butter – You don't actually have to refrigerate butter. Keep it in a covered dish in the cabinet and you'll have perfect, spreadable butter for your toast every morning. Keep some in the refrigerator if you're planning to do some baking, because you don't want your butter to be TOO soft when it comes to cookies and pie crusts. Also, store extra butter in the freezer for up to a year. If you live in a particularly hot or humid climate, though, you may find that keeping butter in the cabinet won't work for you. It doesn't tend to mold, at least not very quickly, but when it gets too hot, it will liquefy, and once it's melted, it's never going to be the same again. Butter **can** "spoil" but I can't say I've had any in my house long enough to find out. But from what I understand, it can start to age like cheese, and when it's done, it will begin to emit an ammonia-like scent, and the milk fats will start to separate. If it's looking lumpy and smelling like cat pee - just throw it out. Then immediately email me and tell me how long you had that butter before it did that because OH MY GOD, HOW LONG DID YOU HAVE THAT BUTTER?

Carrots – You can definitely keep carrots in the refrigerator... but you don't have to. Store them like potatoes. If you WANT to keep them in the fridge, though, take them out of the plastic bag - they do better with some air circulating around them. That's why those bags that they come in have holes in them. But, take them out and they'll last twice as long, at least. Baby carrots dry out faster than their full-size friends, so leaving them in an airtight container with an inch of water is a good way to keep them at their peak tastiness. Change that water every couple days, though, as it will develop an unpleasant slimy texture after a bit. And keep them away from the apples!

Celery – Celery will keep for weeks in the fridge, but it will lose it's crunch. If celery gets a little limp, cut off the dry ends of the ribs and just soak it in some cold water and it'll return to its original crunchy state. This stops working after a while though - if you soak it, and it's still limp, it's time to send it to the compost.

Cheese – Cheeses are living beings, and should be kept cool, but too much cold diminishes the flavor. If your refrigerator has that little cheese drawer, use it. It'll keep things from getting too cold. If not, put them in the crisper. It tends to be less chilly there. If you have a cool, dry pantry, some cheeses can actually be stored in a temperature controlled environment without actually being refrigerated, but for most of us, we don't have storage space like that. Bear in mind, too, that anything called "Cheese Food Product" or "American Cheese" DEFINITELY needs to be refrigerated because while it is a "dairy" product only in the strictest definition of that term, it's not really a cheese.

Chilis/Peppers – Like tomatoes, they tend to wither quickly in the refrigerator. Once they're cut, store them in a plastic bag, or other airtight container. They lose their crunch pretty quickly, but if you're cooking them, that's not really an issue. You really only have a few days before they start to get slimy and unpleasant.

Citrus Fruits – Oranges, lemons, limes, grapefruit, etc. don't necessarily need refrigeration, until you cut them. Leave them in a basket (Not a bowl!) on the counter and they'll be good for a couple weeks. They need air circulating around them and will only start to mold when they don't have air circulating, or if they have trapped moisture between them. Refrigerators trap moisture on the skins, and will accelerate that decay.

Cucumbers – Cold, crisp cucumbers are one of the most satisfying things in the world. But if you refrigerate them, keep them away from fruits like melons, etc. Many fruits (melons, bananas, and others) emit a gas called ethylene that assists them in ripening. Cucumbers are super sensitive to that gas and start to go over-ripe really quickly, and become flaccid, wet and messy.

Eggs – The fastest way to confuse Europeans is to remind them that Americans store their eggs in the refrigerator. That's because in the US, eggs are so aggressively washed before they make it to market, that the naturally protective protein coating (called a "cuticle") on their shells has been washed away, and refrigeration is the only way to keep them fresh - and since they've already been refrigerated, they need to stay refrigerated. They do keep a surprisingly long time in the fridge if they're kept cold, but avoid keeping them on the door. Every time you open your refrigerator, the items on the door warm up fastest. That's why it's okay to keep your condiments and pickles, etc. there, because they can withstand the fluctuating temperature. Eggs are a little fussier though, and don't want that much time in the heat until they're cooked. The upside of refrigeration is that a cold-stored egg can last about 6 weeks. Where in Europe, a non-refrigerated egg is only reliably good for about 3 weeks.

Fresh Herbs – Really, just treat fresh herbs like cut flowers. Put them in a jar with clean, fresh water, and leave them on the counter. If you aren't going to get to them in the next couple days, put them in the fridge in that jar with water. But, replace the water often, as old water accelerates decay. Note that Basil, in particular, does not like refrigeration, even in a jar with water and will wilt, and turn brown very quickly.

Honey – Seriously? Why would you want it cold? Putting it in the refrigerator is the fastest way to make it turn to a grainy mess. Archeologists have found perfectly fine honey in ceramic jars dating back 5,500 years. It can live in your cabinet for a few months.

> **SIDEBAR:** *Most commercially produced honey in the United States is actually high-fructose corn syrup with honey flavoring. Check your labels. And no, it still doesn't need to be refrigerated.*

Hot Sauce – Tabasco and other pepper sauces really don't need to be kept in the fridge. Generally speaking, they don't *want* to be in the fridge. The cold tends to beat down their heat, and causes them to lose their spicy flavor. They'll be fine in the cabinet.

Ketchup – In reality, ketchup keeps fine in a cool, dry cabinet. But if you don't go through it very fast, keep it in the refrigerator.

Maple Syrup – This is another one that blows my mind. If it's a regular grocery store maple syrup, it's going to mostly be corn syrup with some maple flavor, so it can live fine in the cabinet. Same goes with agave syrup. If, for some reason, you have REAL Maple Syrup, however? And I mean ACTUAL, REAL Maple Syrup that costs about 10 times what you paid for that "Pancake Syrup" at the grocery store? Then put in the refrigerator. Just warm it up before you serve it.

Mushrooms – As I mentioned, use those pretty quickly, especially if you're wanting to use them fresh, as in a salad. Cooking will kill off most germs, but while they're sitting in your fridge, they're just little sponges... just soaking up the cooties.

Mustard – Same as ketchup, it's really fine in the cabinet. But refrigerate it if you don't plan on using it up within a week or two.

Onions/Shallots/Garlic – Once they're peeled, or chopped, then refrigerate them. But the layers tend to trap moisture, and once they're in the refrigerator they seem to start molding immediately. Store them like potatoes.

Potatoes – Similar to their nightshade cousin tomatoes, potatoes don't keep well in the fridge. Keep them in the pantry, in a cool (but not cold), dry place, and they'll stay good for weeks. Once they're chopped, keep in the fridge, or use them quickly.

Tomatoes – The fastest way to kill a tomato is to make it cold. They immediately start to decay, wither and taste terrible. Tomatoes keep best on the counter, out of direct heat, and will last nicely for up to a week.

> **SIDEBAR:** Of course, this list wouldn't be complete without the most popular resident of most refrigerators - **Leftovers**. Generally speaking, 72 hours is the limit on most food - even if it's packed nicely in airtight containers. Depending on what it is, the microwave isn't a great way to reheat most leftover food. Pastas can be reheated on the stove (add a couple tablespoons of water), chops, steaks and cutlets can usually come back to life in the oven. But remember - you only have 3 days. Day 1 is usually pretty good, Day 2 is less than amazing, but usually edible and getting to leftovers on Day 3? Only out of desperation. After that, say goodbye to those doggie bags.

- CHAPTER 4 -

Pots, Pans and Tools

After years of cooking and having a kitchen of my own, I've come to realize that I'm a little bit of a gearhead, but only as it applies to kitchen implements. I come from a long line of kitchen tool enthusiasts, so every time a pearl-handled cherry pitter, or Venetian Glass olive boat catches my eye, I have to resist the urge to possess it. Are they helpful? Maybe. Are they necessary? Not really.

Alton Brown, of food television fame, describes these items as "unitaskers" - meaning that they have one thing that they do, and that's it. And sometimes they don't do it particularly well.

Now, I'm not including the most basic of the basics - silverware, dining plates, bowls, etc. It's good to have as many of each of those for as many people live in the house, of course, but it's also a good idea to have enough for your potential guests too. But remember, you're going to have to wash them when they're dirty, and store them somewhere between dinner parties.

As before, I'm breaking this up into *The Essentials* then the *Nice To Haves* and, of course, *The Extras*, for down the road when you're looking to expand your kitchalia collection.

When it comes to some essential tools - the ones you'll use every time you cook - have more than one of each thing. When you're cooking, you don't want to have to wash and re-wash your one silicone spatula over and over while you're working on dinner. Many of these tools are usually sold as sets and, depending on where you're shopping, can be incredibly affordable.

Shop at your local discount stores - Ross, TJMaxx, Marshall's, Target, etc. for these, and also thrift stores. When it comes to pots and pans, it's far better to shop at a thrift store and find a slightly used, but higher quality pan than to buy a brand new piece of junk. Heavy bottom pans are what you're going for. As Anthony Bourdain said in his masterwork *Kitchen Confidential*, "A proper saute pan, for instance, should cause serious head injury if brought down hard against someone's skull." For non-stick pans, though, try to buy new. You can find them used, but if they're in the thrift store, there's probably a good reason the previous owner got rid of it. Any sign of scratches or gouges in the surface, you don't want it. Shop at your local restaurant supplier. Never use metal tools in it, never put it in the dishwasher. Wash it in warm, soapy water, and hand dry it. Take care of it and it will take care of you.

#1
THE ESSENTIALS

Pots and Pans
- 8-10" Non Stick Saute Pan
- 12" Straight Side Skillet
- 2 quart Saucepan
- 9" x 12" Roasting Pan
- 10" x 13" Baking Sheet

Tools
- Measuring Cups and Spoons
- Meat Thermometer
- Medium Whisk
- Flat Grater
- Can Opener
- Heatproof, Silicone Spatulas
- Wooden or Bamboo Spatula and Spoons (Frequently sold as a set)
- 4 oz. ladle
- Potato Masher - Metal
- Metal cooking tongs
- Large Mixing Bowl
- Colander
- Mesh Sieve
- Oven Mitts/Potholders

Knives
- 8" Chef's Knife, or Santoku Knife
- Serrated Bread Knife

#2
THE NICE-TO-HAVES

Pots and Pans
- 6-8 Quart Dutch Oven
- 12" Saute
- Cast Iron Grill Pan
- 10" Springform Pan
- 10" x 13" Pyrex Casserole
- 12 cup Muffin Tin

Tools
- Ice Cream Scoops with release triggers
- Folding Steam Basket
- Mandoline Slicer
- Rolling Pin
- Box Grater
- Sauce Whisk
- Silicone Basting Brush
- Pyrex Mixing Bowls
- Serving Platter
- Serving Bowls
- Salad Spinner

Knives
- Paring Knife
- Large Meat Cleaver (Sometimes called a Chinese Cleaver)
- Flexible boning knife

#3
THE EXTRAS
Pots and Pans
- Heavy Stock Pot (3-4 Gallon)
- ½ - 1 quart smaller Sauce Pan
- 9" Ceramic Souffle Dish
- Wok or Paella Pan
- Non-stick Crepe Pan

Tools
- French Rolling Pin
- Silicone pastry mat
- Bamboo Steamer
- Tortilla Press

Knives
Any others you like

SMALL APPLIANCES

The Essentials
Most kitchens find the basic things super useful - a toaster, a coffee maker (if you like coffee, or plan on having guests who like coffee) but also consider a cheaper French press, then get an electric kettle. It's a speedy way to heat water for tea, coffee, and anything else you need. They heat faster, use less energy than a stovetop kettle, and the ones with the automatic shutoff are safer. These are usually available for $20 or less at any number of discount stores and drugstores.

The Nice to Haves
If you like rice, and plan to have it frequently, pick up an inexpensive rice maker. Of course, if you plan to make a lot of stews and such, maybe a countertop pressure cooker. They also make rice really well. Air fryer? Sure... not necessary, obviously, but they can be convenient for small dinner preparations. An electric skillet is, unquestionably, the best way to make pancakes, but they tend to take up a lot of cabinet space. Do you NEED an electric knife? Well, how often are you carving a roast turkey or ham? They slice bread like a dream, but so will a bread knife.

The Extras
There is a never ending supply of small specialty appliances that you can buy. They promise convenience and speed and endless joy in your kitchen. They can be fun! Those panini press/grills are great, and make a perfectly nice steak. But have you ever cleaned one? Annoying.

Before spending money on anything in that vein ask yourself three things: Where am I storing this thing? How easy is it to clean? How many things can I make in it?

BLENDER vs. FOOD PROCESSOR vs. CHOPPER

If the budget allows, consider an 8-10 cup food processor, a smaller (1½ - 2 cup) food chopper, or a blender. Consider what you want to make most. If you like to make smoothies and milkshakes most, you'll just need a blender - they tend to be cheaper ($30 or under).

But if you aren't wanting to puree everything - maybe you want to make a chunky salsa now and again - consider a food processor with an 8-12 cup bowl. You can also make those smoothies or blended soups in it like a blender would, but it gives you more options. Remember, food processors are truly a "You get what you pay for!" item. You can get some great ones for less than $50 or so, but they aren't going to have as strong of a motor. Perfectly fine for chopping most vegetables, but I wouldn't recommend using it to crush ice or to knead particularly heavy doughs.

There are also the smaller food choppers - they're like baby versions of food processors, and are a great option when you're just looking to make quick work of chopping vegetables. They can usually be had for $20 or less, and are a great option when you're starting out.

There is also a wonderful invention called an Immersion Blender (or Stick Blender) that can be super useful if you make a lot of sauces or blended soups, but it does present unique challenges in terms of both cleaning, and storage. They tend to be too long or thick to fit in most drawers. And they always should be hand washed. But, there are some that come with modular attachments that can double as a food processor - and those might be worthwhile. This, like so much, is an example of "You get what you pay for." If you find one for $20, you'll be lucky if it makes it a year.

MIXERS - Hand or Stand?

Hand mixers are an excellent, relatively inexpensive option when you want to whip up a quick cake mix, or make whipped cream and don't want to whisk it by hand. They can also help smooth out a blended soup, or whip potatoes. But if you're looking for a bigger, stronger machine that can also knead bread for you, look at a stand mixer. KitchenAid®, of course, is probably the high water mark in stand mixers, but they will set you back between $300 and $600 - not to mention the endless attachments and gizmos that you can accessorize with.

The upside, of course, is that the mixer will be with you for decades if you take care of it. Really, that's true of most appliances, pots and pans - if you buy higher quality, and take care of them, they'll last a really long time. But hey, the budget doesn't always allow that, so my advice is always the same - Buy the best you can, within your budget, and upgrade later when you're able. Hand down your old stuff, if it's still usable, and help someone else who's just starting out.

- CHAPTER 5 -

Stock, Sauces and Condiments

Some Food History

THE MOTHER SAUCES

A Weird, And Widely Disputed Bit Of Food History That I Probably Don't Have Entirely Correct

In the early 19th Century, Marie Antoine Carême - the French chef who *kind of invented* modern French food - published several books on cooking at a time when cookbooks were a new and fancy thing that only the cooks that worked for very rich people would have. Carême included in his writing a list of what he called the <u>Four Mother Sauces:</u> *Béchamel*, *Espagnole*, *Velouté*, and *Allemande*.

From each of these formulations, he theorized, dozens of subsequent variations could be made. Then, in the early 20th Century, another very fancy French Chef, Auguste Escoffier, reworked that list - removing the Allemande (because it was really just a variation on velouté that just involved cheese or heavy cream) and he added Hollandaise and Tomato Sauce to that list.

Let's break down Escoffier's five.

Béchamel - The White Sauce
Made with: Milk & Roux

You're already familiar with some variation of béchamel. Ever had biscuits with creamy country sausage gravy? Yeah, that's basically a béchamel, with some extra seasoning and sausage. It's a staple in most traditional lasagna recipes, macaroni and cheese, and a lot of fancier fish dishes. Basically, it's a cream sauce, and a source for a lot of variations.

Velouté - The Velvet Sauce, or Mother of Gravy
Made with: Stock & Roux

The word velouté simply means "velvet" referring to its luscious, smooth texture. Truly, this is the one that you'll probably know best. If you've ever seen someone add cornstarch, or a roux, to a pan of hot broth to make gravy, you've seen a velouté happen. A true velouté, in the Frenchest possible sense, is made from a lighter broth - chicken or fish - that was created from bones that haven't been overly roasted and browned, so it keeps its lighter color and flavor.

Hollandaise - The Dutch Sauce
Made with: Butter & Egg Yolk

There's no real clear reason why it got the name Hollandaise - or particularly why the French called it "The Dutch Sauce" - but the name stuck, and here we are. It is the best saucing option for Eggs Benedict - indeed, I suspect that Eggs Benedict only exists as a delivery system for Hollandaise. Of these five sauces, hollandaise seems to be the most intimidating to try to make, because it tends to be fussy, and prone to breaking. It involves emulsifying egg yolks and lemon juice, and butter, and you have to keep the temperature at a very specific level, and keep the whisk going and it seems like you can only do it with 5 hands. Alas, it's not really that scary. But a hand mixer can come in very handy.

Tomato Sauce - The Red Sauce
Made with: Tomato & Vegetables

Strangely, tomato sauces, as we know them now, are fairly new innovations. Tomatoes didn't make it to Europe until the colonization of what is now known as North and South America in the 15th and 16th Century. Of course upon their arrival in Europe, tomatoes were treated with fear and derision, since botanists (correctly) identified it as being related to the deadly Nightshade/Belladonna family of plants, despite the fact that the Spanish colonizers, while in what is now modern day Mexico, saw the fruit of these plants being utilized in sauce form even then. Indeed, the indigenous people they encountered had been eating tomatoes and making sauce from them since at least the 7th Century CE. The Spanish also brought tomatoes to the islands of the Philippines that they had colonized. From there, they expanded into southeastern Asia into what is now Thailand, Cambodia and Vietnam, and of course into India, China and Korea who have all adapted it into their cuisines to differing extents.

Farther north in Europe, however, tomatoes were slower to find favor. While the French and English thought the plants were beautiful and would keep them as decorative greenery, they weren't interested in eating the fruit. Eventually, Spain and Italy gave it a shot and worked out the first tomato cookery in Europe.

Of course, tomatoes made some people sick - blame, of course, was in great supply, cooks were punished and panic ensued. At that time, rich folks in Europe ate off of pewter. Acidic foods like tomato would leach lead from the plates and people would, understandably, eventually get sick from lead poisoning, and as a result, usually drop dead. Poor people, though, usually ate off of wood planks and bowls, and wouldn't get sick. So, some "scientists" at the time tried to correlate being able to eat tomatoes with being poor and that somehow being rich (remember: wealth, at the time, was thought to be God's will...ugh...) would preclude them from being able to eat them, because their delicate wealthy, overfed digestive systems couldn't possibly manage to eat such a savage fruit. Best to leave them to the poor, they believed.

But in reality, even the rich liked the way they tasted. But, their poshness prohibited them from indulging in them, or even admitting to wanting them. Knowing that there was interest, and that they were easily grown in Southern Europe, cooks in Spain and Italy started to explore it more and began developing new and interesting ways to cook them, learning from Turkish and Moorish cuisine, among others. Once ceramic and glazed china started to gain popularity among the "influential" classes, the number of fatalities from lead poisonings began to plummet, because they SHOULDN'T HAVE BEEN EATING OFF OF PEWTER IN THE FIRST PLACE!

> **SIDEBAR:** *As a note, modern pewter is safe to eat from because it doesn't contain lead anymore. But that's only really been within the last century, so if you have any antique pewter, just leave that on the shelf with the rest of the tchotchkes.*

Eventually, when assorted Habsburg Princes and Princesses married into other families (and sometimes their own, let's be real here...) and ended up sitting on thrones all over Southern and Central Europe, they would bring their own cooks, and their own culinary tastes and traditions with tomato cookery to their new royal courts.

Those tastes immediately became fashionable among their courtiers and the "posh" classes, which worked down to the lower classes and tomatoes took their rightful place in the kitchen among some of the most important culinary staples - from ketchup to marinara and everything in between.

As the great European migration of the 19th Century came to the United States, immigrants from all over Europe started to bring their own recipes and culinary traditions. In the melting pot of the major cities where most arrived, all of these tastes for tomato began to blend and proliferate.

Espagnole - The Spanish Sauce
Made with: Brown Stock, Vegetables & Roux

Espagnole is a very tasty, savory brown sauce, but one that doesn't get used as commonly anymore - at least not in its original form. It would be easy to mistake it for the ubiquitous brown gravy that's such a part of American and British gastronomy, but that's not exactly right either, the major difference being our old friend, the tomato.

The story of the origin of this sauce has a few different versions, each with a different reflection on the impact of migration on European culinary traditions. One commonly repeated version was that in 1615 when King Louis XIII of France married the Spanish Princess Anne (one of those Habsburgs we were just talking about), she brought a retinue of courtiers and cooks, and along with them, exotica like tomatoes and chocolate to the French court from Spain's holdings in the New World.

For their wedding feast, the cooks that she brought with her showed the cooks at the French Royal Court how they used tomatoes and mushrooms in their brown sauce with their roasted meat dishes to give the murky brown meat sauce some much needed punch. It was a smash success and they all lived happily ever after.

Well, not really. By the end of the 18th Century, France would experience its own Revolution, effectively toppling the ruling House of Bourbon, and in the subsequent two centuries, most of the influential families wearing crowns, at the time, died off as the Holy Roman Empire slowly lost political control over their vassal states, while increasingly popular notions of revolution and republic displaced deference to an oppressive, and ever wealthier monarchy. Italy, Spain, Germany, France, Portugal and others formed their own individual republics with representative democracies and have spent the ensuing decades updating borders and trying to perfect this new egalitarian system... Where was I? Oh yeah... Sauce Espagnole.

Over the 20th Century and up to today, the sauce evolved into other different sauces that were more suited to the individual cultures. If you've ever had home-made beef stew that's prepared with tomatoes and wine, HP Sauce - a British staple - or A1 Steak Sauce, or any number of brown sauce type condiments, you'll have a good sense of where it ended up.

I suppose one of the takeaways from centuries of colonization, is the endless ways to boost food's flavor and appeal by adding flavorful sauces, garnishes and condiments. These are the frequently the easiest of things to make, and keep around for, sometimes, a very long time. But they're not usually things that we think to make until we actually want to eat them. Things like stocks are essential to many dishes, and while you can buy them ready-made at the grocery store, it's so easy to make them, and keep them in your freezer until you're ready to use them.

In this chapter, I'm including several that can be made ahead, and some that have to be made to order. But don't be afraid to explore options and adjust flavors to meet your tastes. Why don't we start with one of the most important: **Stock**.

SUPER SIMPLIFIED STOCK

One of the most important staples you can have in your kitchen is a good, flavor-ful Chicken Stock, and/or Vegetable Stock. As I mention in the chapter about stocking your pantry, picking up a few, ready-to-go cartons from the grocery store is a good idea and only makes life easier and unquestionably more deli-cious.

But! If you're motivated to do so, making stock is a fairly easy way to use up scraps, and get the most out of your leftovers. Not to mention the feeling of supe-riority you'll earn when you get to pull your homemade stock out of the freezer next time you're making dinner.

> **PRO TIP -** *Keep a gallon-sized plastic bag in your freezer, and every time you have bones and leftover ends of celery, fennel, carrots and/or onions, throw them in that bag. (Have separate bags for chicken bones, beef bones, ham bones, etc.) Once you have a bag filled and find yourself with an afternoon to play in the kitchen, you can make yourself some delicious stock.*

Now, there will be purists who will be happy to make snide comments about this technique not being as sufficiently French as they want it to be – but that involves much more time. We're looking for an easier route. By the way, have you heard of Bone Broth? Yeah, that's just a fancy word for stock.

Here's a straightforward recipe for making chicken stock. Substitute beef bones, or ham bones as you like. If you're wanting to make a meatless stock, eliminate the bones, and add more aromatic vegetables (celery, fennel, onions, carrots, sweet peppers, garlic, etc.) to your mix. The approach is the same, but can be accomplished in under an hour.

Basic Chicken Stock

What You Need:

Chicken Bones – at least 1 lb., most of the meat removed
4 cups roughly chopped onion
2 cup roughly chopped carrot
2 cup roughly chopped celery *(Fennel is also a nice option and lends a nice sweetness)*
6 cloves of garlic – fresh, peeled, lightly smashed
1 cup chopped fresh parsley
2 Bay leaves
1 Tablespoon of dry Thyme, or three, 5" sprigs of fresh
2 Tablespoon of chopped Fresh Rosemary leaves, or three 5" sprigs fresh
Salt, Pepper

ROAST YOUR BONES!

Preheat your oven to 350 degrees.

Take your freezer bag filled with bones and veggie pieces. Let it thaw for about 15 minutes – just long enough to break apart the frozen pieces. Assess what you have. If you're light on onion, carrots or celery from your freezer bag, add some FRESH to your bag (no pre-cooked in here!). Ideally, you want to have at least 4 cups of chopped onion, 2 cup of carrot and 2 cup of celery. These don't need to be finely minced – in fact, large chunks in this case are better.

Drizzle a few tablespoons of oil (Olive or Vegetable) into the bag, and add your garlic cloves. Roll around the bones and vegetables in the oil until everything is lightly covered. Once it's mixed well, dump it into a roasting pan. Make sure there's enough space so everything can be spread evenly across the bottom of the pan.

Sprinkle 1 Tablespoon of kosher salt (or 1 ½ teaspoons of table salt), and a teaspoon of black pepper across the bone and vegetable mix.

Roast your bones and vegetables in the oven for about 35 minutes. Take your pan from the oven, and stir everything around in the pan. Is everything starting to brown? Put it back into the oven for another 10-15 minutes. Remember, brown = flavor. But if things are starting to turn black, however, pick it out of the mix. Burnt vegetables will make your entire stock bitter. Your bones should look slightly dried out, and browned around the bits of meat and fat still remaining attached, but browning. Your vegetables might look slightly dried out, the onions might look a bit translucent and brown.

MAKING THE STOCK

If you have a stock pot, now's the time for it to shine! (Wash the dust off first.) If you don't have a stock pot, a large (5 quart-ish) pot will work fine.
Turn the heat to high, add the bone and vegetable mix to the pan, and add enough water to cover the top of your bone and veggie mixture. Once the mixture starts to boil, reduce the heat to a simmer, and add your herbs.

Stir it all together. Make a point to use your mixing spoon to dig ingredients from the bottom, and move them to the top. Let it simmer on low, uncovered, for 30-40 minutes until you can see the water levels start to reduce. Scoop out the bones and vegetables – throw them away. They no longer have the flavor they once did - they've given it all to the stock - and don't taste like much anymore.

Let your stock simmer for another 15 minutes at the lowest simmer setting.

Strain out your stock by pouring it through a fine mesh sieve into another pan, or a large mixing bowl. You're looking to take out any errant pieces of bone or vegetable and make your stock as smooth as possible. Rinse out your original pan to remove any residual bits from the bones and vegetables.

Return your strained stock to the pan, and continue simmering on very low heat, uncovered for another 15 minutes. Small bits of foam, and particles will start to float to the surface. Skim those off as it simmers.

Remove the pan from the heat, and let it rest and cool for about 15 minutes. As it cools, the residual fat will start to collect at the top – gently skim off the fat with a spoon. Pour the stock into a large mixing bowl, and put it in the freezer for about 10 minutes (set a timer!), remove from the freezer, skim off the fat that's collected at the top, then refrigerate. After the stock has cooled completely in the refrigerator, (leave it overnight if you can), your stock will likely have taken on a gelatinous consistency - Don't be afraid, that's a good thing!

Remove the remaining fat that has collected at the top (it's perfectly okay if there's some fat bits left in there), then use your stock or freeze in an airtight container. If you choose to freeze it, I VERY MUCH recommend labeling the container with the date and the flavor. I once made chicken noodle soup with what I THOUGHT was chicken stock, but turned out to be ham stock. I'm not saying it wasn't delicious, but it WAS unexpected.

Stock keeps nicely in the refrigerator for 3-4 days, or for up to a year in the freezer.

Béchamel Sauce

This one is going to come up as an ingredient in a few dishes in this book. Once you get this recipe down, your macaroni and cheese game will jump to serious new levels.

What You Need:

4 Tablespoons of Butter
4 Tablespoons of Flour
2 Cups of whole milk (or 2% if you must)
A pinch of nutmeg (optional, but does add an interesting boost of flavor)
A pinch of salt

In a smaller saucepan, melt your butter. When your butter just starts to bubble, add your flour. Mix your flour into your butter, and roll it around the bottom of the pan until it's all well mixed. Congratulations! You just made a roux! Let this cook on a low/medium heat for another minute. As the flour cooks, and the gluten heats, it will start to relax, and become softer. You'll also notice it starting to darken.

Once it's darkened slightly to a pale golden color - like the color of a golden labrador retriever - add your milk, and grab a whisk. You'll start whisking the milk and flour mixture, smashing out the lumps and keep whisking until it's smooth. Reduce your heat if it starts to bubble too much. A low simmer should be enough.

Keep whisking, and don't let the bottom of the pan start to burn. As you're stirring, the sauce will start to thicken. Add a pinch (⅛ teaspoon at most) of nutmeg, and your pinch of salt. Mix well, remove from heat, and now it's ready to serve! You can leave it in the pan, off the heat, for a while if you're working on macaroni and cheese - but it will thicken a bit. You can also refrigerate it and come back to it later, but bear in mind that it will thicken up considerably.

When you go to reheat it - please, don't microwave it - gently reheat it in a pan, and add some milk, a tablespoon at a time, until the sauce comes together.

Multiply the recipe as needs be - these measurements will yield about two cups of finished béchamel.

Serve over steamed vegetables, or over potato slices for a brilliant baked gratin.

Hollandaise Sauce

Wait to make your hollandaise until you're ready to use it. Once it's made, it doesn't like to sit for long.

What You Need:
4 egg yolks (Save the whites for breakfast)
½ cup melted butter (one stick)
1 Teaspoon of Dijon mustard (the smooth kind, not grainy)
1 Tablespoon of lemon juice
A pinch of cayenne (optional, but delicious)
A pinch of salt

Put a medium sized saucepan on the stove with about 2 inches of water in it. Turn the heat to medium.

In a metal mixing bowl, whisk your egg yolks, Dijon mustard and lemon juice just until they start to turn pale yellow and begin to increase in volume. While the water on the stove is starting to simmer, set your mixing bowl to the top of the saucepan. Reduce the heat on the water to low. This is the temperature control part - you don't want the water to touch the bottom of the bowl. You just want the steam to gently heat it.

In a thin stream, add the melted butter to the yolk mixture, continuing to whisk the entire time. Go slow with the butter, and keep that whisk moving! When all the butter is added, remove it from the steaming water pan, whisk in the salt and cayenne. Everything should be nicely emulsified through, and your sauce should be glossy, yellow and still thin enough to be poured. Serve immediately.

PREP NOTES - *Problems that can come while making hollandaise:*

Is it lumpy? *Sounds like your egg yolks started to scramble. Your steam pan is probably too hot. Unfortunately, there's no going back from here and saving it. Just start over and try again!*

Does it look oily and separated? *Ah, the ever-present threat of broken hollandaise is upon you. Is your melted butter cooled off too much? Or did you add too much too quickly? Keep whisking and see if the sauce comes together. Add a ¼ teaspoon of hot water to the mixture as you're whisking - sometimes that can help bring the butter into the egg yolks. Don't add too much too quickly or you'll end up with scrambled eggs. It'll still be delicious, but won't be that smooth, creaminess you want.*

Sambal

Sambal is a spicy chili/garlic sauce, and is a staple of Southeast Asian cuisine. It is a marvelous addition to soups, curries, rice and even sandwiches. There are also about a million versions of sambal, so it's something of a Choose Your Own Adventure sauce. Here is a fairly basic, medium-spicy recipe that gives you a nice starting place - feel free to riff with flavors and spice as you like.

What you need:
    8 red serrano chilis
    1 medium red bell pepper (baseball size)
    ¼ cup minced garlic
    2 Tablespoons vegetable oil
    ½ cup vinegar (plain white vinegar, or rice wine vinegar)
    2 Tablespoons salt
    1 Tablespoon sugar

Slice your peppers vertically, and remove the stems and seeds from the peppers. (Don't touch your eyes, and immediately wash your hands!) Put all of the ingredients into the blender or food processor, and chop until you reach a fine blend, but not entirely pureed smooth. A little texture is good. (But even if it's smooth, it's pretty delicious). Store in an airtight jar in your refrigerator. Leave it for a few days to let the flavors blend together. The taste will intensify as it stays in your refrigerator..

PREP NOTES - *If you want to make a milder version, instead of serrano chilis, replace them with Italian Sweet Fry Peppers. Ready to take it hotter? Add a red jalapeno as a replacement for one of your serrano chilis. Keep adding jalapenos to add heat as you wish.*

Parsley Pesto

Traditional Genoa style pesto is made with Genovese Basil and pine nuts, but this bright, fresh-tasting type is a delicious variation that can be used on any number of dishes - including on pasta, pizzas, sandwiches. If you want to make the traditional Basil variety, just substitute Basil for the Parsley, and pine nuts instead of almonds or walnuts.

What You Need:
½ cup blanched almonds or unsalted walnuts
½ teaspoon of kosher salt (or ¼ teaspoon of table salt)
½ cup. shredded parmesan
2 Tablespoons minced garlic
4 cups roughly chopped Flat Leaf Parsley
½ cup olive oil (use the greenest, most "extra virgin" you have)
½ teaspoon ground black pepper

As preparation goes, this one doesn't get much easier. Just put everything in the blender or food processor, and blend until fairly smooth. You can also smash everything together in a pestle and mortar - indeed, the word "pesto" comes from the Italian word meaning to pound.

You may need to open your chopper and scrape down the mixture a couple times, so everything can be thoroughly blended. If your mixture is still too clumpy, chunky or dry, slowly drizzle additional olive oil until it reaches a creamy, but spreadable texture.

Like it's basil-based sibling, this keeps nicely in the refrigerator for 3-4 days, but you can store it in the freezer for up to a year.

PREP NOTES - *You can adjust the garlic, and the choice of nuts to suit your own taste. Almonds and walnuts tend to be mild, but earthy. Pine nuts are sharper in flavor, which suits basil pesto perfectly, but with the parsley, I tend to think there's too much in the top flavor notes, but not enough warm middle flavors. Toasted hazelnuts are also perfect in the recipe.*

Tzatziki

Truly, if Ranch Dressing had an Old World ancestor, this could be it. It dates back to, at least, the 19th Century Ottoman Empire, and has since spread variations throughout the Mediterranean and The Levant. This is another incredibly simple recipe that is always a crowd pleaser. You probably already know it as the delicious cool sauce on a gyro, but you can serve it as a dip on a veggie platter or with potato chips, or use it as a spread for any sandwich. It's the perfect thing to throw together at the last minute when you need a delicious little something on the side.

What You Need:

1 cup plain yogurt (full fat is best)
1 medium cucumber
2 cloves of garlic
½ cup finely chopped fresh dill (or 2 tablespoons dried dill, but it IS better with fresh)
1 tablespoon lemon juice
½ teaspoon kosher salt

Cut off the stem and blossom end of the cucumber. Peel your cucumber, and slice it lengthwise. Using the tip of a teaspoon, scoop out the seeds and pulpy core - throw the seeds and pulp away. Using a cheese grater's large holes, grate the cucumber into a separate bowl. Add your salt to the cucumber, and gently stir it through. Let the cucumber rest for about 10 minutes, then strain out the excess water.

Gently squeeze out as much moisture as you can, without crushing the grated cucumber. In the bowl, add your yogurt, garlic, dill, and lemon juice. Fold the ingredients together gently until well mixed. Your finished tzatziki will have some texture from the shredded cucumber and dill. Refrigerate for an hour or so, at least, before serving. It will keep in the refrigerator for several days in an airtight plastic or glass container.

Garlic Basil Aioli

Aioli is really nothing more than a fancy variation on mayonnaise with a garlic finish. It's a perfect finish for baked salmon, goes great on roasted vegetables, and is probably my favorite thing for french fries. This recipe has only six ingredients, but it does require a little more technique. It doesn't hurt to have an extra set of hands, or a stand mixer with a whisk attachment.

What You Need:
1 cup olive oil
5 peeled, whole garlic cloves, smashed
2 large egg yolks, at room temperature
2 teaspoons freshly squeezed lemon juice
8 basil leaves finely chopped, or 1 Tablespoon of dried basil
½ teaspoon kosher salt
Large Mixing Bowl and a Balloon Whisk, or a mixer with a whisk attachment

Start by making a garlic-infused olive oil. Pour your olive oil and garlic cloves into a small saucepan - set it on a medium/low heat for 12 minutes or until the garlic cloves start to sizzle (whichever comes first!), then remove it from the heat. Stir the garlic through the oil. Pour the oil and garlic cloves out of the hot pan and into a bowl, or a 2 cup glass measuring cup. Set it aside, and let it rest and cool for about 45 minutes.

> **SIDEBAR:** *This garlic-infused oil is super useful to have on hand for most of your olive oil needs. You can make a bunch in advance and keep it on hand. Keep it in an airtight bottle or jar in your cabinet for weeks.*

Once your oil has cooled to room temperature, remove your garlic cloves and mash them into a paste with a fork, and set them aside. Separate your eggs, save your egg whites in an airtight container and refrigerate - save them for breakfast. Put your yolks into your mixing bowl, with the salt, basil, and lemon juice. Turn on your mixer (whisk attachment!) or start whisking. Go slow, and gently mix those ingredients together.

Now, to start the emulsion. As you're mixing the yolks and other ingredients, slowly add the olive oil, drop by drop. As you're whisking, add a drop of oil, and once it's well incorporated, add the next drop of oil. Continue doing that. DON'T STOP WHISKING! Once you've added about half of the oil, your mixture should start looking creamy, and become a pale yellow. At this point, you can add the rest of the oil in a THIN stream as you continue whisking. When the last of your oil has been added, you're done! Fold the mashed garlic cloves into your aioli, distributing evenly throughout the mixture. Scoop out your aioli and put it into an airtight container. Your aioli will keep in the refrigerator for 2-3 days, but is best eaten within 24 hours. This recipe will yield about 2 cups of aioli, so if that's more than you'll use within that time, just cut the recipe in half.

Marinara Sauce

A good marinara is the basis of so many delicious dishes. This is a fairly simple version that I've developed over the last 20 years that I've used on pasta, chicken parmigiana, and served with fried vegetables. You can use fresh tomatoes or canned, but I'd recommend using canned if you've never made it before. Canned tomatoes are delicious, and take far less time.

What Your Need:

    3 tablespoons of olive oil
    4 lbs. Fresh Roma Tomatoes, or 3 lbs. Canned Crushed Tomatoes
    5 Peeled Fresh Garlic Cloves
    ½ cup robust red wine
    1 teaspoon Ground Black Pepper
    2 teaspoons salt
    ½ teaspoon sugar
    10 leaves of fresh basil, chopped

If you're using fresh tomatoes, give yourself more time. You'll want to core and peel the tomatoes before they cook. Using a paring knife, cut around the stem end of the tomato, pop it out, and then slice off the bottom. Drop your tomatoes into simmering water for 20 seconds, then drop them into iced water. The heat, then extreme cold will cause the skins to pucker, and come off easily. Squeeze out most of the watery pulp and seeds.

In a large, heavy-bottom pot, add your olive oil and garlic cloves. Turn your heat on to medium heat. Stir the garlic cloves around in the olive oil until they start to brown slightly. Add the tomatoes to the pot, and stir them thoroughly. Add your salt, pepper, sugar and red wine. If you're using fresh tomatoes, use your spoon to crush the tomatoes into chunks. As they cook, they'll soften more.

Reduce your heat, and simmer on medium/low heat for about 30 minutes. Every 10 minutes or so, stir your sauce, scraping up from the bottom. After your sauce has reduced for 30 minutes, taste your sauce. Does it need more salt? Add more (¼ teaspoon at a time!) and taste it again.

Remove your sauce from the heat. Chop your basil leaves into a fine mince - stir it into your sauce. Stirring around your sauce, find your garlic cloves. Remove them from the sauce - smash them into a paste, and stir the garlic paste into the sauce.

Use the sauce immediately, or store it in the refrigerator or freezer. Marinara will keep in the refrigerator for a few days, or in the freezer for about a year.

Giardiniera

This is a marvelous, and unique relish that I discovered while living in Chicago, as it is a staple of Italian Beef Sandwiches. During this time, I also discovered that there are approximately one ZILLION versions, in varying degrees of spice, and fineness of texture. There's also a pickled snack version that isn't minced to relish size, but instead left as chunky vegetables in a spicy, vinegar brine. Both are spectacular. This is the fine chopped relish version, in a "mild/medium" flavor level. Obviously good on a sandwich, but also delicious tossed with pasta and grilled fish, Italian Sausages, hot dogs, chips, grilled chicken...

It isn't a particularly difficult recipe, but this does take four days before it's ready to eat, so plan your time well.

What You Need:

Day One:
4 celery stalks, minced fine
2 medium carrots, minced fine
1 small onion, minced fine
2 green bell peppers, diced
2 red bell peppers, diced
6 fresh serrano chili peppers, diced
½ head of cauliflower (enough to make about 1 ½ cups when chopped down)
1/2 cup kosher salt

Day Two:
8 cloves garlic, finely chopped
1 cup small green olives (with the pimento stuffing)
1 cup white vinegar
1 tablespoon dried Italian Seasoning
1 teaspoon red pepper flakes (add more if you like additional heat!)
1 teaspoon black pepper
1 cup olive or vegetable oil (ideally, something fairly neutral in flavor)

Finely chop, or chop in the food processor all of the vegetables on the Day One list. When cutting the peppers, make sure to remove all of the pith and seeds. If you're using the food processor, don't chop them too small - you'll want your pieces to be about ¼" in size, so there's still some texture to them. Place all the finely chopped vegetables into a mixing bowl, and pour enough cold, clean water to just reach the top of the veggies. Add ½ cup of kosher salt (or ¼ cup of table salt) - mix the salt in. Cover the bowl with plastic wrap, and refrigerate for at least 24 hours.

Once time has lapsed, pour off the water by pouring the mixture into a large, fine sieve. Gently rinse off the vegetable mixture to remove the excess salt. Return the mixture to the bowl.

Finely chop your olives (again, food processor, or by hand), and add those to the veggie mix. Add your garlic. Mix everything thoroughly.

In a separate bowl, mix your vinegar, olive oil, Italian Seasoning, red pepper flakes and black pepper. Whisk these together, then pour over the veggie mixture. Mix thoroughly - using your hands is the best way to feel if everything is mixed together, and to ensure that there are no clumps of vegetables.

Cover your bowl, or portion the mixture into a few airtight, plastic containers and refrigerate. Leave the mixture in the refrigerator to marinate for at least two days before serving. It will keep in the refrigerator for weeks, but I tend to use it up before that much time passes.

Vinaigrette

At the heart of every marinade, is a vinaigrette realizing its potential. This simplest of salad dressings is simply an emulsion of oil with vinegar or a citrus juice, and seasonings of some sort. The variety really knows no limit. The conventional wisdom around vinaigrette is that the ratio is 3 parts fat/oil to 1 part acid/vinegar. When whisked vigorously, this can emulsify into a stable mixture that won't easily separate when served. Of course, you can shake that ratio up with differing results which are perfectly delicious. Just because your vinaigrette separates doesn't mean it isn't tasty. This recipe is a jumping off point - add seasoning, and experiment with flavors you like.

What You Need:

1 ½ cup olive oil
½ cup vinegar
1 teaspoon dry Italian Seasoning
½ teaspoon kosher salt
Pinch of black pepper

Add all ingredients to a mixing bowl, or into your food processor.

> **SIDEBAR:** *I often keep a jar that pickles or pasta sauce came in to use as a shaker for salad dressings. You can also buy a bottle or jar for this purpose, but they come free when you buy pickles - just saying...*

Mix the ingredients together. If you're whisking by hand, whisk aggressively. Or shake it in a jar until it's well blended. Keep it in an airtight container, and it'll keep for ages.

Variations on a Theme

Vinegar - You can use any vinegar you like here. Balsamic is a classic, and apple cider vinegar is fantastic on a salad of bitter greens. Even replacing the vinegar altogether with citrus juice is a marvelous flavor boost. If you want to keep it sweeter, you can use sherry, or any wine in place of the vinegar. A champagne vinaigrette is truly magnificent!

Seasonings - Substitute the Italian seasoning blend with minced green onions, or other fresh herbs and finely chopped sweet peppers. Subtler herbs tend to get lost under the vinegar flavor though - think strong flavors like oregano, thyme, marjoram, etc.

When it comes to oil, I think the greenest, most "extra virgin" olive oil tastes better. But if all you have is canola oil you can make perfectly delicious vinaigrette. Avoid things like corn or peanut oils - they bring too much of their own flavor and can throw off the delicacy of the taste.

Salsa Rojo

When I was very young, my mom and I spent summers canning, and one of the best things she made, and canned, was salsa. We had a massive garden, and always had more tomatoes, chilis and onions than we knew what to do with. Salsa was an easy way to make use of those vegetables, and create something that everyone loved. Here are two that I still make, 35 years later.

What You Need:

2 lbs. Roma or Beefsteak tomatoes, peeled & cored
1 large white onion
4 cloves garlic, peeled and chopped
2 jalapenos
2 Anaheim chilis
1 green bell pepper
2 teaspoons kosher salt
2 tablespoons of vegetable oil
2 teaspoons cumin
2 teaspoons paprika
1 tablespoon lime juice
½ cup chopped cilantro
½ cup chopped green onion

Start by coring and peeling your tomatoes. Squeeze out most of the seeds and gelatinous goo in the middle. Peel and rough chop the onion. Cut all of the peppers vertically, remove the stems, seeds and pith. Chop them roughly.

The food processor can be very helpful here. Use it to chop the onions, peppers and tomatoes to smaller, but still chunky pieces. You can also do this by hand, but it will take a bit longer. When those are ready, put a large saucepan, or pot on the stove. Turn your heat to high, add your oil and onions. Once your onions start to sweat, and begin to turn slightly translucent, add your garlic. Once your garlic starts to warm, add the peppers, tomatoes, salt, cumin and paprika. Once your pot is starting to bubble, turn your heat down to simmer.

Stir everything together, and let your sauce simmer. If it starts to boil, reduce your heat until it's just simmering low, with small bubbles coming up the sides of the pan for 20 minutes. The color will darken slightly, and will reduce as the water cooks off.

Remove the pan from the heat, stir well, and let the salsa rest in the pan, on the stove, for about 15 minutes. Mix in the lime juice, cilantro and green onion. Taste the salsa at this point. Does it need more salt? Add pinch by pinch until it tastes the way you want it.

Salsa Verde

This is an amazing variation that I still make in huge quantities and can for myself and friends. Here's a recipe for a smaller batch, that will make your enchiladas so much more than you ever expected.

What You Need:
3 lbs. green tomatillos
1 large white or yellow onion
8 cloves of garlic
4 Anaheim chilis
2 jalapenos
½ cup chopped cilantro
¼ cup fresh squeezed lime juice
Kosher salt
Ground black pepper
Vegetable Oil

Preheat the oven to 350 degrees.

Start with your tomatillos. If they have the dry husks, peel them off, and throw them out. Cut the stem-end cores out of the tops, and drop your tomatillos in a large bowl of warm water - this will help remove some of the residual sap left from the husks. And you don't have to peel tomatillos! Cut the peppers vertically, and remove the stems, seeds and pith. Peel and roughly chop the onion. Drain the water from the tomatillos.

Add the peppers, onion and garlic to the tomatillos in the mixing bowl. Drizzle vegetable oil across the tomatillos and peppers. Toss and roll everything in the bowl until the oil is evenly distributed across the vegetables.

Line a 9" x 12" roasting pan with foil. Pour your oil-coated vegetables to the roasting pan. Sprinkle the veggies with a teaspoon of kosher salt and ½ tea-spoon of black pepper. Roast in the oven for 30-45 minutes or until the tomatillos are completely softened.

Remove the pan from the oven, and let it cool. Once it's cool enough to touch with your hands. Pour the veggies into your food processor and blend until smooth. You may have to puree the vegetables in batches, if it gets too full. Pour the pureed salsa into a large saucepan or pot (just make sure you have 2-3" open space between the top of the salsa and the top of the pot.)

Cook your pureed salsa on a medium heat for 15 minutes, while mixing. Remove from heat, and allow to cool for about 15 minutes. Add the lime juice and cilan-tro.

You can use your salsa immediately, or store it in the refrigerator for a few days. Salsa verde does freeze pretty well, so you can keep it frozen for about a year. Once you've thawed it out, mix it really well before you use or serve it.

Guacamole

Truly one of the most popular and ubiquitous appetizers, and happily it's ridiculously simple to make. You don't need, or really even want, a food processor. It's all just a matter of mixing and mashing with a fork. This is a milder spiced version, but if you want to add some heat, just add a finely minced jalapeno to the mix. Serve with tortilla chips or with fresh vegetables.

What You Need:

4 large avocados (pitted, scooped, and chopped into chunks)
½ cup sour cream (Really, this is optional, but I like the creamy texture)
½ cup finely chopped white onion
¼ cup lime juice
1 cup diced tomato (the canned sort, drained, is perfectly okay here!)
½ cup chopped green chilis (the mild, canned version)
1 teaspoon cumin
1 teaspoon garlic salt
½ teaspoon ground black pepper

Start by mashing your avocado until it's in smaller chunks. Then fold in everything else, until well combined. Serve immediately.

> **NOTE:** *If you're refrigerating your guacamole, tightly wrap with plastic wrap - trapped air causes the guacamole to turn brown.*

- CHAPTER 6 -

Soup

Any time someone has asked me to teach them about cooking, I start with soup. If there is any sort of secret to the making of soup, it's just about layering flavor, and knowing when to add ingredients to make sure everything cooks evenly. Firm vegetables like carrots and parsnips go in early - they take the longest to cook, but you also want the onions in early so they dissolve into the broth. Soft herbs, noodles, etc. are added at the end so they don't disappear entirely... make sense? Those basics are true of all cooking - if you're truly a complete noob, soups are where to begin.

One of the many great things about making a huge pot of soup is that you tend to have leftovers - and having quarts of soup are the best way to have easy meals ready to go, just waiting in your freezer after work.

French Onion Soup

*This is another incredible classic soup that has a million subtle varia-
tions, but the basic formulation is pretty consistent. When I was in
France, I was surprised by it's ubiquity. For some reason, I just assumed
that it was some Americanization that no one in France would actually
eat - it's possible, perhaps that it was on offer just to the tourist trade,
but I didn't mind. Even the least amazing of the ones I had were still
pretty good. This is my adaptation of the version I learned to make.
Rich, dark, and delicious. When a recipe is this straightforward, and
involves so few ingredients, it's a good time to indulge a bit. Spend a
couple extra dollars for really wonderful Gruyère, and a nicer bottle of
wine - doesn't have to be crazy expensive, just a slightly better version
can make all the difference in the world.*

What You Need:

6 White Onions, sliced into ¼ inch slices
2 Tablespoons minced garlic
1/2 cup of Butter *(one stick)*
1 Tablespoon dry thyme leaves, or two springs of fresh thyme
1 bay leaf
¼ teaspoon ground black pepper
2 Tablespoons flour
1 cup dry red wine *(Burgundy, Cabernet, etc.)*
2 quarts beef stock *(your own, or packaged)*
½ lb. grated Gruyère or Swiss cheese, or slices
1 baguette, sliced into ½ inch slices

In a large saute pan on medium high heat, melt your butter, then add your onions, garlic, thyme, bay leaf and pepper. Saute the onion mixture until they start
to become soft and darkened into a deep caramel color. Sprinkle flour over the
onions, and stir around for about a minute until the flour is well cooked into the
onion. Add your wine, and scrape the bottom of your pan.

Transfer the mixture to a large soup pot on medium heat, and stir to loosen up
the mixture. Add your beef stock, and bring the heat back up to a fast simmer
for about a minute, then reduce heat to low. Stir, and let simmer on low for an
additional 15 minutes. Turn on your oven's broiler, or oven to 350 degrees. Remove the bay leaf, and sticks from the thyme (if you used fresh.)

Turn off the heat, and ladle the soup mixture into oven-proof bowls, or oven-
proof stoneware soup crocks - make sure your onions are evenly distributed. On
the top of the soup, float two of the baguette slices (bottom against bottom, to
create a rounder shape) and sprinkle a generous amount of cheese on top of the
floating bread. Set your soup bowls on a baking sheet, and put under the broiler
for about 2-3 minutes, or in your oven for 10-15 minutes, or until the cheese is
melted and bubbling brown. Remove from the oven and serve immediately with
the extra baguette. It's a magnificent starter, or as an entire meal.

Spicy Carrot Bisque

This is, for me, a near perfect winter soup. It's one you can pour into a thermos, sit by a fire and drink from a cup. It's warming and rich, but still light and bright in flavor. The other incredible thing about this recipe, too, is that it freezes like a dream. You can make quarts and quarts of this ahead of time, and it'll be just as fresh and delicious tasting as when it was first made. It's also an easy adaptation to vegan with just a couple easy tweaks. This is also easiest with a blender to smooth your soup - not impossible to do without one, but definitely takes a little more effort with a potato masher and a whisk. You can also use a hand mixer.

What You Need:

2 lbs Carrots, peeled and chopped into large chunks
1 Red Bell pepper, seeds and stem removed, roughly chopped
1 medium white onion, roughly chopped
2 Tablespoons Olive Oil
1 teaspoon kosher salt
¼ teaspoon black pepper
1 teaspoon cumin
½ teaspoon smoked paprika
2 Tablespoons minced garlic
1 bay leaf
¼ cup minced fresh ginger, or ginger paste
4 cups vegetable stock, plus one cup of water
½ cup half and half
¼ cup finely chopped flat leaf parsley
One lemon, zested and juiced
½ cup whole milk or half & half

Preheat your oven to 400 degrees. Toss your carrots, bell pepper and onion in the olive oil. Sprinkle with salt, and roast in a 9" x 13" baking pan for 30-45 minutes, or until the carrots are soft enough to insert a knife easily.

While your vegetables are roasting, heat a large soup pot with your vegetable stock, cumin, paprika, bay leaf, garlic and ginger. Bring to a fast simmer, and reduce heat to a low simmer. When your vegetables are roasted, add them to the soup pot and stir. Remove from the heat, let the soup rest for 30 minutes, uncovered.

Remove the bay leaf. Using an immersion blender, or hand mixer, slowly mix everything - pureeing everything until smooth. If you only have a blender, you CAN scoop the soup into the blender - only fill the pitcher HALF full, and loosely hold the lid. Your soup will be HOT, and WILL splatter if you fill it too much. Blend it in batches, until it's done. I DO NOT recommend this method if you're new!

Turn the heat back on under the soup pot, stir in half and half, parsley, lemon zest and lemon juice. Let it come to a low simmer, and remove from heat. Stir in milk. Let it rest for about 10 minutes before serving.

The Easiest Chicken Noodle Soup
That Didn't Come in a Can

This is another fabulous opportunity to use up leftover roasted chicken, but you can easily poach a couple chicken thighs, or a few chicken legs, if leftovers aren't available. Also, whether you have chicken stock from Chapter 5 made and waiting in the freezer for you, or have cartons of "ready to go" stock, taste your soup as you go for salt. Sometimes store-bought stock is REALLY salty, so there's no need to add very much. Truly, this is one of the easiest things to make and have a few days worth of very satisfying meals. Also, look at this recipe as a jumping off place for a million other soups. Instead of chicken, consider meatballs, and instead of the noodles, add chopped spinach, etc. etc. etc.

What You Need:

- 2 cups leftover chopped chicken or 2 Chicken Thighs, *poached or steamed*
- 1 medium white onion, fine chopped
- 1 cup celery, fine chopped
- 1 cup carrot, fine chopped
- 2 cups fideo, or vermicelli broken into 1"-2" pieces
- 2 quarts chicken stock
- 1 Tablespoon vegetable oil
- 1 Tablespoon dried oregano
- 1 Tablespoon minced garlic
- 1 teaspoon ground ginger
- 1/2 teaspoon ground black pepper
- ½ cup finely chopped parsley

In a large pot on medium flame, heat your vegetable oil, then add your onion, carrots and celery. Sprinkle with a pinch of salt, and saute until the vegetable mixture starts to brown slightly.

Add your chicken, Italian seasoning, garlic powder, ginger and black pepper. Stir the seasoning until it's well distributed throughout the mixture. Add your stock - stir well, and increase your heat to high. Let your stock come up to a simmer, ALMOST to a boil, and let simmer for about 15 minutes. Cut your heat to VERY low, cover the pot, leaving a small vent for steam to escape, and leave it for about 10 minutes.

Stir it again, then spoon out a little bit to taste. Does it need more salt? Add pinch by pinch until it's salty enough for you. Stir. Add your fideo or vermicelli, and stir well for about 20 seconds. Let it continue to simmer for about 5 minutes. Remove from the heat, add your parsley - allow to rest for 10 minutes before serving.

Baked Potato Soup

If you like richer, more substantial soups this may be the mother of them all. I suppose you COULD technically call this a stew, but do the semantics really matter when it's this delicious? This is one of the few that I wouldn't necessarily freeze - not that anything bad really happens to it, but sometimes it can separate a bit, and be slightly less velvety... But who cares! This is always a crowd pleaser!

What You Need:

3 lbs Russet Potatoes, cut into 1" cubes
1 medium white onion, finely chopped
2 ribs celery, finely chopped
½ cup green onions, finely chopped
1 lb. bacon, chopped
2 quarts vegetable stock
1 cup half & half
1 cup sharp cheddar cheese, grated
½ cup mozzarella cheese
½ cup parmesan cheese
¼ cup flour
1 Tablespoon vegetable oil
1 Tablespoon Italian Seasoning
1 teaspoon kosher salt
½ teaspoon black pepper

Heat your oven to 350 degrees. Set aside 3 strips of bacon, and roast the rest of your bacon for approximately 30 minutes, or until they're well browned and crispy. Remove the bacon from the sheet to cool and drain over paper towels. Once cooled, crumble into bacon bits.

On the baking sheet that your bacon came from, spread out your diced potatoes. Sprinkle the potatoes with salt and pepper, and bake them for about 20 minutes in the bacon grease.

Chop the three strips of bacon that you set aside into small pieces. Brown them in a large soup pot, over a medium heat - add your onion and celery. Once your onions start to become slightly translucent, add your flour and Italian Seasoning, and stir until you have a lightly browned roux. Let the mixture dry a bit until it's a thick paste, then add your stock. Stir vigorously to work out any flour lumps that may be in the roux.

Once your potatoes have been in the oven for about 20 minutes, give them a fork test - does a fork easily cut into a piece of the potato? Even if it's slightly still firm, remove them from the oven, and drain off the bacon fat. Add the drained potatoes to the pot, and stir them through the stock mixture. Some of the potatoes will start to disintegrate - THAT'S OKAY! - bring the heat up to high just until the mixture starts to bubble - then reduce it quickly to medium/low. Let it simmer for about 15 minutes. Stir thoroughly, and stir in your half & half, then your cheeses, reduce your heat to low.

Simmer on low for 5-10 minutes, and remove from the heat. Let the soup thicken somewhat, and serve with chopped green onion, bacon bits, cheese, croutons and anything else that sounds good.

Freeze extra soup for up to 6 months.

Beef Barley Soup

Truly, this is a "feed the masses" recipe. The richness of the beef and bulk of the barley make this a VERY filling meal, so a little goes a long way. Serve with warm, crusty Italian bread and butter on cold winter nights.

What You Need:

1 lb.. beef chuck roast, or "cowboy" steaks, cut into 1" cubes, or smaller
1 cup chopped onion
1 cup chopped carrot
1 cup chopped celery
1 cup chopped mushrooms
2 quarts beef stock
1 cup dry barley
½ cup red wine or vermouth
1 tablespoon Worcestershire sauce
1 bay leaf
2 garlic cloves
1 teaspoon dry marjoram
Salt and pepper

In a large pot, over medium heat, warm a tablespoon of olive or vegetable oil with your onion, celery, mushrooms and carrots. When your onions just start to turn pale golden color, add your beef and garlic. Sprinkle with ½ teaspoon of salt and pepper. Stir until everything is browning, then add your wine. Let the wine bubble, and dislodge any brown bits from the bottom of the pan. Scrape the bottom of your pan and stir the brown bits in. Add your stock, bay leaf, Worcestershire sauce and marjoram. Stir well.

Let your stock come up to a bubble, then reduce heat to low. Stir again, and put the lid on the pan, slightly ajar to let steam escape. Let the soup simmer for about 15 minutes. Stir in your barley, and let it simmer a further 15-20 minutes, or until your barley is cooked through.

Stir again, and taste for salt and pepper. Adjust seasonings to your taste. Once the barley is cooked, and the soup is seasoned to your taste, turn off the heat, and put the lid back on the pot. Let the soup rest for about 15 minutes before serving.

Broccoli Cheddar Soup

This is such a rich, wintery soup that you'll want it around all the time. This is also a recipe that's super easy for you to adapt with flavors that you like. Don't like beer? Leave it out. Like cauliflower more than broccoli? Use it instead. You can make it spicier with the addition of a little chili powder, or crushed red pepper. Serve with crusty bread and butter.

What You Need:

2 tablespoons olive oil
4 slices of bacon, roughly chopped
1 large onion, finely chopped
1 cup finely chopped celery
1 cup finely chopped carrot
1 cup finely chopped green onion
4 cups finely chopped broccoli (frozen is also okay!)
¼ cup flour, sifted
1 quart chicken stock
½ cup milk
2 cups sharp cheddar cheese, shredded
2 cups Monterey Jack Cheese, shredded
4 oz. cream cheese (half of a block)
12 oz (approximately) of beer (Ale, lager or even an IPA)
1 Tablespoon garlic powder, or 2 Tablespoons of fresh minced garlic
1 Tablespoon dried Italian Herbs, or Oregano
½ teaspoon black pepper

In a food processor, or very patiently with a knife, chop down your broccoli until it's chopped very fine. Stems should be no larger than ½" on any side. A few blitzes in the food processor will make short work of this.

In a large pot, start sautéing your bacon and olive oil over medium heat. Add your onion, celery and carrots once your bacon starts to brown. Stir everything together. As your onions start to sweat and become translucent, add your broccoli and stir completely. Sprinkle the garlic, Italian Herbs and pepper, and stir throughout. Then, add your flour to the mixture. At first, the mixture will become dry, then the flour will start to brown. Add your beer, stock and milk. Stir throughout.

Then add your cream cheese and shredded cheeses. Stir thoroughly as the cheeses melt - make sure the cheeses are well incorporated. Reduce your heat to low, and let the soup simmer for about 15 minutes. The soup will thicken as it simmers. Once it's as thick as you like it, remove from the heat, stir in your green onions, and serve. Garnish with croutons, more green onions, bacon bits, more shredded cheese, sour cream or any other things you like.

Ridiculously Easy Vegetable Soup

This recipe is really just something of a framework to jump off from - use veggies that you like! I also like to add either wild rice or barley to this recipe so it has a little extra heft. It's an excellent soup to make a TON of in advance and freeze for later. Just remember, dense vegetables should go in the pot first, because they take longer to cook. You can certainly use frozen veggies for this one - they don't take nearly as long to cook.

What You Need:

2 Tablespoons Olive Oil
2 Tablespoons minced fresh garlic
1 onion, chopped
4 ribs celery, chopped
4 carrots, chopped
1 medium potato, peeled and diced into ½ inch cubes
1 cup sweet peas
1 cup diced tomatoes, drained
2 quarts vegetable stock

4 cups Napa cabbage, cut fine
2 cups green beans, cut to 1"
2 cups sweet corn kernels
Juice from 1 lemon
1 cup fresh parsley, minced fine
1 Tablespoon dried Italian Seasoning or Oregano
2 bay leaves
1 teaspoon paprika

In a large pot, saute your onions in the olive oil over medium heat. Add a teaspoon of salt to the onions as they brown. Once your onions start to become translucent, add your celery, carrots and potatoes. Cook until they start to brown. Add your garlic, paprika and Italian Seasoning, and stir into the vegetables. Add your stock, and bay leaves. Bring the broth to a simmer.

Add the rest of your vegetables to the pot, and another teaspoon of salt. If you want to add 1 cup of barley or rice, this is the time to do it! Stir everything together - once the pot comes back up to a simmer, reduce the heat to low, and let it simmer for about 15 minutes.

Using a fork, test the potato and carrot for doneness. Taste your broth to see if it needs more salt. If it does, add ¼ teaspoon of salt at a time until it tastes right. If they're softened adequately, then everything else will be ready. Reduce your heat to low, and prepare any garnishes you want to add - croutons, sour cream, shreds of parmesan, etc. all add some deliciousness.

Remove your bay leaves, stir in your parsley and lemon juice then serve. If you're freezing some, ladle out the amount you want to freeze into another shallow pan, to help it cool faster. Once it's cooled, transfer to an airtight container to freeze. It will keep in the freezer for about a year.

- CHAPTER 7 -

Appetizers, Dips and Snacks

Truly, the things that I love most to both make and eat, almost all fall into the category of appetizers. Small plates of tasty things, dips and snack-like things you can eat in one or two bites. Mostly I appreciate it for the variety of textures and tastes, and I don't have to commit to one large entree that I may end up regretting. Indeed, some of the most enjoyable dinner parties I've ever thrown have been little more than a buffet of appetizers.

At any cocktail party you're having, or any time you're entertaining more than just a few people, it's a good idea to consider what the maximum impact for the least effort might be. Two very simple options are: A meat and cheese plate, and crudités (the fancy French name for a veggie platter). A striking arrangement of beautiful fresh vegetables, and interesting cheeses offer a visually exciting option for grazing. It might be a bunch of work beforehand, but at least you won't have to keep running back and forth to the kitchen when you'd rather be spending time with your guests.

MEAT & CHEESE/DELI PLATTER

At any grocery store, you can easily pick up an overpriced tray of cheese slices and sandwich meats. But for a cocktail party situation you may find it cheaper and much more interesting to pick out a few cheeses, a couple of interesting meats, and arrange them nicely on a platter for a far more entertaining option. Be careful here, though. The meat and cheese platter is a really fast way to blow the budget if you aren't paying attention to price tags - frequently grocery stores will price cheeses by the HALF pound, so it doesn't seem quite as expensive as it actually is when you ask for a pound. But, also bear in mind, a pound of cheese is a LOT of cheese.

Here are some suggestions on where to begin:

Cheese Choices: Variety is the key, and so is knowing your audience. Are your guests adventurous eaters? Or are they intimidated by those aggressively flavored, cave-aged, slightly basement-flavored cheeses?

One Familiar Firm Cheese - this should be something that isn't terribly intimidating to the uninitiated. It could be a nice sharp cheddar, a smoked gouda or a medium age manchego. Manchegos are particularly nice here, because they seem exotic to the uninitiated, but aren't at all scary.

One Soft Goat Cheese - there are a lot of options here. From pretty much any major grocery, you can find an interesting log of goat cheese with any number of flavors infused into it. Find something that isn't too firm that can be spread with relative ease on a cracker.

One Soft, French Rinded Cheese - this can be a little adventurous. I like a strong Camembert, or even a young Brie. These, too, can be acquired from your local market for a reasonable price.

One Wild Card - this one is entirely up to you. I LOVE blue cheeses. A simple Danish blue, or a crumbly Gorgonzola. But if your guests are a more adventurous foodie sort, consider an Époisses, potted Stilton or even a Limburger. Or, if you want to go simpler, look for an Emmenthal, or similar firm Swiss cheese.

Meat! Meat! Meat! *Vegetarian? Skip this part.* Much like with the cheeses, consider who you're feeding. The culinary neophyte might be scared of Capocollo or a duck terrine, but most carnivores love a salami.

Prosciutto - It can be a little expensive, depending on where you're shopping. But the slices tend to be a bit large for cracker purposes. Cut the paper-thin slices into 4 or 6 smaller pieces, and ruffle them a bit on the platter. If it's entirely cost prohibitive, look for thin sliced deli ham and treat it the same.

Salami/Sopressata - Salami comes in a million different varieties and flavors. I tend toward a spicier sopressata-type version, but there is no shortage of milder, and more herbaceous flavors widely available. Pepperoni is also an option here, if you're trying to keep the budget under control.

Paté/Rillettes/Terrine - Thanks to grocery stores being able to satisfy the expanding global palette, there is a world of interesting patés available, ready to go, at the deli counter. If you're interested in delving a little deeper, specialty grocery stores carry pork and duck rillettes in jars that are absolutely magnificent. They're a little more expensive, but well worth the occasional splurge - both in financial cost and calorie intake.

In addition to the meats and cheese, who are obviously the stars of the show here, you'll want to include a couple types of crackers (relatively inexpensive), perhaps grissini - those pencil thin breadsticks, and/or a baguette, sliced into rounds and toasted ever so slightly. Consider including a handful of grapes, strawberries, sliced pears and apples, and if you're feeling terribly extravagant, include an unusual jam or honey. Perhaps a fig or date jam? They go brilliantly with strong cheeses. Maybe a French grain mustard?

CRUDITÉS

Much like the meat & cheese platter, this can be readily picked up from the grocery in a ready-to-go format, but the markup on them - just to have someone cut things up for you - is absurd. Not to mention the fact that they're usually a little dried out, and rarely very interesting. And that cup of barely considered ranch dressing with the peel off top? Ugh. Not that there's anything particularly wrong with ranch dressing - it does go well with veggies, after all, but is that the only option?

The FAR better, cheaper and fresher option is to buy the veggies, and cut them up yourself, and mix up some interesting dip or hummus to accompany them. Now, if you're very skilled with a knife, you can certainly make those radish rosettes, and carrots that look like palm trees, but it's certainly not a requirement.

Thankfully, such overly fussy and unnecessary fanciness has largely fallen out of fashion. Sit this platter next to your cold dips (recipes for those later in this chapter!) Here are examples of what I like to include - pick and choose as your tastes dictate, and add any veggies you like that you like:

Celery Sticks - Cut each rib of celery in half VERTICALLY, then cut into 3-4" long sticks.

Carrots - Either baby carrots, or cut into sticks roughly the same size as your celery sticks. You can also sometimes find the smaller rainbow variety with the tops. Peel the skin, chop down the green tops, and cut them in half vertically - they look stunning served on a veggie platter.

Tomatoes - Grape or Cherry Tomatoes, cut in half vertically. Assorted colors certainly add some flair.

Broccoli/Cauliflower Florets - Definitely a matter of taste. I love the appearance and texture both on the plate and as they're eaten. If you want, a very fast blanching (20 seconds in boiling water, then in ice) can help take away some of the sulphurous flavor that many find objectionable. Chill them well before you serve.

Olives - Really, this can be any kind or kinds you like. I tend to choose the sort that are pre-pitted for this purpose - Kalamata, stuffed green and black olives are all perfect.

Pickles - Small, two-bite cornichons or gherkins are great. If wine is central to your dinner party, though, skip the pickles and olives, as the vinegar-y flavor will really mess with the palettes of your guests when they take the next sip of wine. Truly ghastly.

Cucumber - Relatively thick (¼"?) slices make for easy dipping.

Endive Leaves - Just slice the bottom ½" off the head, and separate the leaves. They make handy little spoons for dips!

Bell Pepper Spears - A combination of red, yellow and orange add much needed color to your platter.

Pickled Cherry Peppers - These are particularly tasty stuffed with herbed goat cheese.

Radishes - Cleaned with their little tail roots removed, cut in half vertically, or into quarters. And yes, if you really want to make those little radish roses, knock yourself out.

Jicama - These are a little unusual to most American palettes, but they're fantastic palette cleansers. They look like big fat potatoes - just peel them, and cut them into ¼ - ½" sticks, 3-4" long. Soak them in a mixture of water with salt, and a splash of white vinegar for an hour.

FOUR QUICK AND EASY COLD DIPS

Here are some quick-prep dips for those moments when you're having people over, or need to bring something to a potluck and don't have a lot of time or money to make it happen. Each of these can be served with any crackers you like, or with a vegetable plate, and can be done relatively inexpensively. Frankly, these are also super delicious spread on a sandwich.

Creamy Goat Cheese Dip

6-8 Oz. Plain Goat Cheese
½ Cup Sour Cream Or Plain Yogurt
3 Green Onions, Chopped
1 Jar Diced Red Pimentos (Usually about 4 Oz.)
¼ Cup Finely Chopped Fresh Parsley
1 Tablespoon Lemon Juice
½ Teaspoon Garlic Powder
Pinch Of Salt

Just mash and mix everything together. Refrigerate for up to a day before serving.

Chili Cheese Dip

1 Cup Sour Cream
1 Cup Grated Cheddar Cheese
½ Cup Mayonnaise
1 Cup Black Beans (Drained And Rinsed)
1 Cup Canned Diced Tomatoes (Drained)
½ Cup Diced Pimentos (Small Jar, Drained)
½ Cup Minced Green Onions or
¼ Cup Minced Chives
1 Teaspoon Mild Chili Powder
½ Teaspoon Ground Cumin

Drain your canned vegetables. Mix your sour cream, cheddar cheese and mayonnaise first, add your chili powder and cumin. Mix thoroughly. Fold in the green onions, beans, tomatoes and pimentos. Chill for an hour or so before serving. Delicious on tortilla chips!

Spicy Feta Dip

1 Cup (8 Oz.) Feta Cheese Crumbles
½ Cup Sour Cream Or Plain Yogurt
½ Cup Pickled Pepperoncini Or Yellow Banana Peppers, Chopped Fine
½ Teaspoon Dried Crushed Red Peppers
½ Teaspoon Dried Oregano (Or Italian Seasoning)
¼ Teaspoon Garlic Powder
¼ Teaspoon Ground Black Pepper

Mix everything well. Refrigerate for a couple hours to let all the flavors come together. Garnish with banana pepper rings, or finely sliced green onions.

Crab Dip

1 Can Lump Crab Meat (6-8 Oz)
8 Oz Cream Cheese (Softened)
2 Tablespoons Sour Cream
3 Green Onions, Chopped
½ Cup Celery, Minced Fine
½ Teaspoon Garlic Salt
½ Teaspoon Paprika
¼ Teaspoon Ground Black Pepper

Mix together everything except the crab. Once everything is smooth, fold the crab in gently. If you overmix, the crab will be mashed down and will break into tiny pieces. You'll want it to have a little bit of texture. Leave refrigerated for at least an hour before serving. Garnish with minced chives.

TWO MARVELOUS HOT DIPS
THAT DON'T REQUIRE MUCH EFFORT

Buffalo Chicken Dip

2 Cups Shredded Chicken (An excellent chance to use up leftovers!)
8 Oz Cream Cheese (Softened)
2 Cups Shredded Mozzarella
¾ Cup Frank's Red Hot Buffalo Sauce
½ Cup Chopped Celery
½ Cup Blue Cheese Crumbles

Preheat your oven to 350 degrees. Mix together the cream cheese, mozzarella, shredded chicken and the buffalo sauce, then bake in a dish until it's bubbling and brown - about 25-30 minutes.

After it's baked, garnish with the blue cheese and chopped celery. Serve in the baking dish with toast points, or tortilla chips.

Spicy Queso Fundido

8 oz. Chorizo tube (It's in most grocery stores, near the bacon or deli meat)
1 can diced tomatoes with green chilis, drained
8 oz. Chihuahua Cheese, shredded (mozzarella is a fine substitute, if Chihuahua is unavailable)
8 oz. Pepper Jack
¼ Cup Milk
¼ Cup Chopped Green Onions
1 large jalapeño, chopped fine (Optional, but nice if you want to go spicy!)

In a medium saucepan, over a medium heat, cook your tube of chorizo. Soyrizo is also a great option here if you're feeding vegetarians (obviously not for vegans, what with all the cheese...) Once your chorizo is browned and the fat is largely separated from the meat, drain off the excess fat, return it to the pan. Add the can of tomatoes and chilis, and the jalapeno (if you're using it.) Once your tomatoes have warmed, and are starting to soften, add your cheeses and milk. Stir gently, but constantly until your cheese has melted. If your mixture is too thick, add more milk, a Tablespoon at a time, until it thins out. Once the mixture is mixed well, add your green onions, and remove it from the heat. Pour it into a large serving bowl, and garnish with chopped cilantro, and a dollop of sour cream. Serve with tortilla chips, but it's also really good with celery sticks.

Devilled Eggs

The vintage-y, retro-ness of devilled eggs are part of what makes them so damned charming and fun. There are also many, many possible variations and there's almost no way to make them bad. Here's my base recipe - feel free to adjust and change flavors to your liking.

What You Need:

12 Large Eggs
½ cup mayonnaise
½ cup cream cheese *(Smoked Salmon variety is marvelous in this recipe)*
3 Tablespoons of dill relish or minced gherkins
2 Tablespoons of finely minced white onion
1 Tablespoon Dijon mustard
¼ cup fine minced fresh dill
½ teaspoon garlic salt
¼ teaspoon paprika
¼ cup chives (finely minced), for garnish *(optional)*

BOILING EGGS: Fill a large cooking pot to about halfway with cold water. Gently add your eggs, turn your heat to high. Once your water is boiling, cover your pan and turn off the heat. Set a timer for 11 minutes. While your eggs are cooking, half fill a large mixing bowl with iced water. Once the timer is done, remove the eggs from the hot water and drop them into the iced water, and stir them around the cold water for a moment. Leave the eggs in the cold water to chill for 20 minutes, or until you can hold one in your hand without feeling any warmth coming from the egg. Peel your cooled eggs gently - softly rolling the egg, with a little pressure to leave a crackle all over the egg shell and deftly peel it away. Once the shell is peeled away, rinse the egg again to remove any residual chips from the surface of the egg. Rest the peeled eggs on a clean towel.

Slice the eggs vertically. Pop the yolks out of the halved eggs, and deposit them into a medium sized mixing bowl. To the yolks, add the softened cream cheese and mayonnaise. Mash everything with a fork, and blend until the yolks are no longer clumpy. You can also use a hand mixer to make quick work of these.

Fold in the remaining ingredients and mix until smooth. Spoon the mixture into the emptied egg whites, or use a piping bag to fill them. Once they're all filled, sprinkle the minced chives across the top to garnish, and/or garnish with paprika and/or chives.

HOT TIP: *You can create a piping bag using a zip storage bag. Fill the bag with your yolk mixture, then snip off a ½ inch corner and squeeze the filling from the bag.*

Hummus

This is one that you have a world of flexibility in preparing. Add to it an endless variety of delicious flavors and spices. It definitely helps to have a food processor to make this easier, but can also be achieved through a patient hand and a potato masher.

SIDEBAR: *One quick note about tahini: Tahini is a paste made of sesame seeds, sort of the texture of a natural peanut butter, but more expensive. Tahini is a "nice to have" item, but isn't cheap to buy just for one purpose. If you eat a lot of hummus, it might be worth it, but you can substitute unsweetened almond or cashew butter for the tahini, or even greek yogurt if you want a delicious, super creamy version.*

What You Need:

1 Can Garbanzo Beans, drained *(14-16 oz.-ish)*
¼ Cup Tahini *(or other substitute!)*
2 Tablespoons lemon juice
2 Tablespoons olive oil
2 cloves garlic, finely minced
½ teaspoon cumin
½ teaspoon garlic salt
¼ teaspoon paprika

This is another one of those recipes that you can throw into the food processor, and just blitz until it's all smooth. No food processor? No worries. Just mash up the garbanzo beans and mix away. When it's smoothed out, serve with a drizzle a tablespoon of olive oil across the top, and sprinkle a pinch of black pepper and chili powder to garnish.

HOT TIP: *Instead of paprika, try this with Za'atar Spice - it's a marvelous spice blend that usually combines savory herbs, sesame, and sumac powder. It's a staple throughout the Eastern Mediterranean and the Middle East, and has a number of varieties. Truly marvelous and can be found in most specialty spice markets, or can also be found relatively inexpensively online.*

Spinach And Artichoke Dip

I think if I have a "signature" dish that I make, this MIGHT be it? It is the one that is most requested for potlucks, and whenever we're having people around, my husband always finds a way to let me know how nice it would be to have on the table, (you know, for the guests!)

If you want it to have a little more spice, I recommend using pepper jack cheese instead of the mozzarella - but either way, I think you'll enjoy adding this to your repertoire.

What You Need:

1 package frozen spinach (8-10 oz.)
1 can (12 - 16 oz) artichoke hearts in water (Do not use the ones marinated in oil!)
1 cup mayonnaise
1 cup shredded mozzarella
½ cup shredded parmesan, plus an additional ¼ cup for topping
½ cup cream cheese (softened)
¼ cup breadcrumbs
1 Tablespoon of garlic, finely minced
½ teaspoon kosher salt
¼ teaspoon ground black pepper

Preheat your oven to 375 degrees.

Thaw your spinach completely, and wring out as much water as you possibly can. Drain the water from the artichokes, and roughly chop them into small chunks - separate the leaves as much as possible.

In a mixing bowl, combine the mayonnaise and the cheeses. Once they're combined, mix in the breadcrumbs, garlic, salt and pepper. Then mix the spinach and artichokes in.

Once it's well blended, pour it into a well buttered baking dish - I usually use an 8" souffle. Sprinkle the additional ¼ cup of parmesan on the top, and a sprinkling of breadcrumbs.

Bake uncovered in the middle of your oven until you see browning and bubbling around the edges - usually about 35-40 minutes.

Fried Pickle Chips

This is a tasty, salty pub snack that is so, so good with beer, and always reminds me of summertime for some reason. It's almost unconscionable that you'd eat these anywhere except out on the back porch. This recipe involves very few ingredients, but like with all breaded and fried foods, it's a little messy to make. But very, very worth it.

What You Need:
One 32 oz. jar of pickle slices (Obviously, more if you want more...)
2 cups of flour
2 eggs
1 Tablespoon of milk
2 cups breadcrumbs (Panko breadcrumbs are really nice here!)
1 tablespoon dry Italian Seasoning
1 tablespoon garlic powder
1 teaspoon chili powder
1 teaspoon ground black pepper
1 quart of vegetable oil for frying

Start by draining your pickle slices. Lay them out flat on a clean kitchen towel. Lay another clean kitchen towel on top and gently roll the two towels with the pickles between them. Don't squeeze too tightly - you're just looking to get most of the moisture off the surface of the pickles. Unroll your pickles, and remove the top towel. Let your pickles continue to air dry.

Pour your frying oil in a heavy bottom pan, and turn the heat to medium. It will take approximately 10 minutes for your oil to warm sufficiently.

Start your breading station! You'll need one, gallon sized food storage bag, and two bowls (soup bowls will work fine.) In the plastic food storage bag, add your flour, garlic powder, chili powder and pepper - close the bag, and give it a shake to mix the ingredients. In the first bowl, add your two eggs and the milk. Scramble the eggs in the first bowl. In the second bowl, add your breadcrumbs and Italian seasoning - mix them together.

Set up an assembly line with your bag of flour & spices first, then your scrambled egg bowl, then your breadcrumb bowl. At the end, have a clean plate, or baking sheet.

Take a few of your pickle chips and drop them into the flour. Shake them around until they're well coated with flour. Remove them one by one, gently shake off the excess flour, and dip them in the egg mixture. Coat it well with egg and shake off the excess. Then coat it in your breadcrumb mixture until it's thoroughly breaded, then lay it on the plate to rest. Repeat until all your pickle chips are breaded.

Drop them in batches of 8-10 in your hot oil and fry them until the crust is nicely browned - this should only take about a minute per batch. Don't overcrowd the pan, or they won't cook evenly. Remove them from the hot oil, and leave them to rest on a plate lined with a paper towel. Sprinkle lightly with salt to taste. (They're already pretty salty, so use your judgment.)

Serve with a creamy dip of your choice - bleu cheese or ranch, or just sour cream with a little bit of hot sauce mixed in.

PRO TIP: *This is a great recipe for pretty much any fresh vegetables that you like, too: mushrooms, zucchini, cauliflower, and green tomatoes in particular are great. They'll tend to take a little longer to cook, or in the case of denser veggies (carrots, etc.) it helps to blanch them for 30 seconds or so in boiling water before you bread them - just let them dry and cool before breading them.*

Baked Brie in Pastry
with Strawberry & Rosemary Compote

This is one of those quick ways to impress at any dinner party, but it's seriously nowhere near as complex as it seems like it should be. I'm including the recipe for the pastry part, but if you used store-bought pie crust, seriously, no one would care or know the difference.

What You Need:
1 Round of Brie (This can really be any size you like, you just have to make enough pastry to wrap around it.)

Pastry
2 cups flour
1 stick of very cold butter, plus 3 tablespoons
1 teaspoon salt
1 Tablespoon of sugar
½ cup cold water

2 eggs, for egg wash

Topping
½ cup chopped fresh strawberries
1 Tablespoon sugar
1 Tablespoon of finely chopped rosemary leaves

Let's start with the pastry. If you have a food processor, now's the time to bring it out. You can also, easily, do this by hand. In a bowl, pour in your flour, salt and sugar and mix them together. Cut the butter into small cubes, and drop them into the flour. With your hands, you're going to squeeze the butter into the flour. Either way, the simplest way to do this, is to just grab handfuls of the butter and flour mixture and rub it between your flat hands. Keep doing this, over and over, until the butter seems to disappear into the flour, and you're left with something like the texture of soft, damp sand. If you're using a food processor, pulse until you reach this texture. Add your water bit by bit, and mash, knead and mix until you achieve a soft ball of dough. It can still be a little rough looking at this point. Wrap it in plastic wrap, or put it in a covered bowl in your refrigerator for half an hour.

Preheat your oven to 350 degrees. Next, onto the topping. In a small saucepan, mix your strawberries, sugar and your chopped rosemary. Turn on a LOW heat, and let the strawberries soften a bit. Mix it all together until the sugar is dissolved, and smash the strawberries into smaller chunks. Simmer for 2-3 minutes over a low heat, stirring frequently. Once the fruit has thickened somewhat, remove from the heat and set aside. It will thicken more as it cools.

Take your pastry out of the refrigerator, and cut it in half. On a lightly floured board, roll one half of your pastry out into a circle. It should be about ¼" thick.

In a small bowl, scramble your two eggs, with a tablespoon or so of water. Brush your egg across the top of the pastry.

Set your brie in the middle of the pastry. Spread your strawberry mixture on top of the brie. Fold the pastry circle up around the brie. Roll your other half of pastry and lay it across the top. Press the pastry down on the top and sides. Cut around the bottom of your pastry and press out any bubbles. On the top of the brie, cut an X in the middle. Fold back the four points, leaving a hole opened on top. Move it onto a greased pan, then brush the egg wash liberally all over the outside of the pastry. Bake for approximately 30 minutes. Once the pastry is thoroughly browned, though, it's done - even if 30 minutes haven't passed. Serve warm - cut into wedges like pie, eat with a fork.

Enjoy the praise your guests will laud upon you.

Stuffed Dates

The first time I made these, I'm not sure I'd ever seen them done, but it seemed like the logical and right thing to do. It was around the holidays, and I'd received this glorious fruit and cheese basket, and part of the basket was this package of the most beautiful Medjool Dates I'd ever seen - plump and sweet perfection! While dates are sweet, they complement strong, salty cheeses quite well. You can also eliminate the bacon, and use a sweetened mascarpone cheese with honey and pistachios in the stuffing for a more dessert-like treat.

What You Need:
24 Pitted Dates
6 oz goat cheese (the herb-coated variety is nice here, too!)
12 Slices of bacon
1 tablespoon of thyme leaves, minced, or 1 teaspoon dried thyme
Pinch of black pepper
24 Toothpicks (without the frilly tops!)

Preheat your oven to 375 degrees.

Start with your bacon. Cut the 12 slices in half, across, to make 24 shorter pieces. Using your knife, gently scrape along the surface of the bacon slice to stretch it into a thinner, longer piece. Now, to the cheese. Mash your goat cheese in a bowl to soften it - add a sprinkle of pepper, and your thyme. Mix until it's softer and creamier.

Either by hand with a spoon, or using a piping bag, fill the cavities of each of the dates with the goat cheese. It doesn't have to be perfect, there can be some cheese on the outside - it's totally okay! Now, roll each of those filled dates into a slice of bacon, and spear each with a toothpick to anchor the bacon in place. Bake on a parchment lined baking sheet for about 20 minutes, or until the bacon is cooked to your liking.

These are a nice pass-around hors d'oeuvre, or can sit nicely on a buffet for a while at room temperature. I've never had leftovers to see what they were like cold, but I'd imagine they couldn't be too bad.

Pimento Cheese

This is one of those distinctly Southern dishes that has as many formulations as there people who make it. As I understand it, it was a good way to use up leftover chunks of cheese when they were too small to use in other dishes, or too awkward to slice for sandwiches. This spread is fantastic just on bread as a cold sandwich, or as part of a hot ham & cheese.

What You Need:

2 Cups grated Sharp Cheddar (the SHARPEST you can find...)
¾ Cup Mayonnaise
½ Cup grated kosher dill pickles
½ Cup minced sweet red pimentos
1 Teaspoon prepared horseradish* (Really, it's optional, but I LOVE the heat that it brings)
½ Teaspoon ground black pepper

Again, this is another easy one to just throw everything into a food processor, if you have one handy. But if you're doing it by hand, chop down the grated cheese to a fine chop until it starts to stick together, then fold everything together until it's well blended. I recommend refrigerating it overnight to allow all the flavors to amalgamate, but it's still pretty tasty after chilling only an hour or two.

Serve on crackers, toast, or with celery sticks.

Refrigerator Pickles

As much as I enjoy canning pickles, sometimes, I don't want to make the kitchen into a steam room - especially at the height of summer when it's approximately one million degrees outside - so I'll just make this cold process version, instead. It's a slightly different version that has a fresher, lighter flavor since it isn't cooked, so I try to shove as much flavor into the jar as possible. Bear in mind, this version should be refrigerated - hence the name. This recipe is to make one quart of pickles, so feel free to scale up depending on how much you want to make.

What You Need:
6 Persian Cucumbers (English cucumbers will work here, too, just count one English for two Persians)
2 Cups White Vinegar
2 Tablespoons minced garlic
¼ cup Fresh Dill - roughly chopped
1 Tablespoon Kosher Salt
1 Teaspoon Black Peppercorns
1 Teaspoon Citric Acid or 2 Tablespoons Lemon Juice

Cut ½" off each end of your cucumbers, and halve your cucumbers vertically. You can cut these down to be as long as you like, you just want them to fit in the jar. If you prefer spears, cut these in half, vertically, again.

SIDEBAR: If you prefer chips, instead of spears or halves, cut them at least ¼" thick, otherwise you'll have thin, floppy pickles... not that there's anything wrong with that. You do what you want!

Pack your cucumbers into your jar - spears and halves vertically, chips layered flat against the bottom. Pack your fresh dill on top of the cucumbers.

In a small saucepan, add vinegar, garlic, peppercorns, citric acid and salt. Warm this mixture only until JUST warmed (140 degrees?). Allow to cool slightly, then pour lukewarm mixture over the dill and cucumbers in the jar. Put your lid on the jar loosely, give the contents a gentle swirl. Refrigerate.

The next morning, tighten the lid, invert the jar, and turn it upright again. In about 2 days, the pickles should be ready to eat. This is one of those marvelous things that get better and better the longer it sits in the refrigerator.

Crab Rangoon

This utterly non-Chinese, non-Thai snack is somehow a staple of Chinese and Thai restaurants all over the US. It is also, probably, my favorite appetizer of all time - it's at least in the top 5. When you're shopping for crab, surprisingly, canned crab meat is probably the best option for this recipe. It's going to be chopped a little finer, so the texture will be a little smoother. If you like a more toothsome texture, go for the fresher, non-canned option, or the Kosher, faux crab version.

What You Need:

1 package wonton wraps (approximately 4" x 4")
1 can lump crab meat
4 oz. cream cheese
1 teaspoon garlic salt
½ teaspoon ground ginger
4 green onions, chopped
Vegetable oil for frying

In a mixing bowl, soften your cream cheese by letting it sit on the counter for about an hour. Mix in all of your seasonings and onions. Once that's well mixed, fold in your crab - you don't want to mix too aggressively, because you don't want to mash up the crab too much. Put this filling mixture into the refrigerator for about 30 minutes.

Step 1

In a large pot, add vegetable oil until you have about 1-1 ½ inch layer of oil in the bottom. Turn your heat to medium/high, and heat until you reach about 350 degrees Fahrenheit, or until you can drop a piece of the wonton wrap into the oil and it starts to fry immediately. This usually takes about 10 minutes, depending on your stove.

Step 2

Now, set up your assembly station. Set a small bowl of cool water at the top of your work area, and open your package of wonton skins.

Take a wonton wrap, and set it on your surface so it's in a diamond shape - the corners pointing top to bottom and right to left. Take your filling from the refrigerator, and spoon 1 teaspoon of filling into the center of the wonton skin. Dip the tips of your index fingers into the water bowl, and wipe the water around the perimeter of the wonton - this will help your wonton seal shut. Fold the wonton skin top to bottom until the points meet. Gently squeeze out the air trapped inside the wonton, start in the middle next to the filling and push out to the edge to seal the wonton closed, squeezing out as much air as possible.

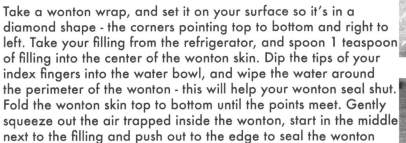

Step 3

Step 4

Next, dab a small bit of water on the right and left points, and bring them together at the top of the filling lump, folding the edges of the wonton around until they make a boat-like shape. Squeeze the points together until they stick. Move the wonton to a plate. Repeat until you're out of filling or wonton skins.

At this point, you can freeze the wontons, or start frying them. They only take about 20-30 seconds in the fry oil. Once they're golden brown, remove them from the oil and set them to drain on a paper towel-lined plate.

Serve with sweet and sour sauce, soy sauce or any condiment you like.

If you're freezing them for later, spread them out on a parchment lined baking tray or other freeze-proof plate for about 3 hours. Once they're frozen solid, transfer them to a large freezer bag. They'll keep in your freezer for up to six months.

- CHAPTER 8 -

Salads

When it comes to a leafy green salad, my reaction is usually a resounding "meh" or maybe, "Oh, okay." Now, I like a salad as much as anyone, but rarely have I had a salad and been so impressed by it that I'd want to go back to THAT restaurant and get THAT salad because it was SO amazing.

As a child of the 70's and 80's we certainly HAD salad, but it really wasn't until the 1990's that salad in the Midwest started to become a real "thing" or meal, unto itself - except, of course, for the ever-present salad bars at a million restaurants, or the sad pile of iceberg lettuce, "bacon" bits and an unidentified, overly-sweet dressing that arrived before dinner at every restaurant. However, when I was a young adult, and started working in restaurants in the 90's, the notion of a salad as a complete meal emerged. Suddenly, you could throw a piece of chicken on a pile of greens and some barely considered vegetables and it magically became a complete meal! Then, interesting new vinaigrettes emerged, and we learned that you could grill romaine and radicchio.

These innovations made them more tasty, sure, but still they weren't always particularly interesting or innovative. Not to mention the illusion that was being pushed that it was always the healthiest option on the menu. After all, if you just take some lettuce, throw on some vegetables that you liked, then boom! You're eating healthy! Right? Well, not really. The explosion of varieties of bottled salad dressings would take your "healthy" calorie count and quadruple it (or more!) - because most processed, bottled salad dressings had a STAGGERING amount of salt & sugar, or worse yet, the ubiquitous high-fructose corn syrup.

> **SIDEBAR:** Go look in your refrigerator now at the label of a mass market salad dressing and be horrified by the sugar content. While you're there, look at the fat content. What sort of fat is involved? Is it olive oil, or dairy? Or something synthetic? Remember, if it's "Sugar Free" it's probably high fat or high salt. Fat free? Yeah... look at that salt or sugar content.

I recall a particular chain restaurant in the late 90's having a section of their menu devoted to "Healthy Options" and on that menu was a massive salad that contained romaine lettuce, corn, black beans, a handful of fried onions, some croutons, orange cheese but also a FRIED chicken cutlet, and a "Tex Mex" dressing that seemed to be a mix of salsa, sour cream, and sugar because it was shockingly sweet. It's a good thing that this was a time well before restaurants were obliged to print out nutrition or calorie content on their menus. There's no way that this monstrosity clocked in at less than 1,000 calories. Was it delicious? Oh, heavens yes. Healthy? Well... I suppose it was a good thing that we were eating vegetables at all.

People were still convinced that they were living a healthy life by eating only salads and asking for everything on the side, as a means of attempting to control what they were eating. This "on the side" trend was popularized by a well known weight loss business, and a number of daytime talk shows at the time.

As a waiter in these restaurants, I observed this particularly annoying habit that was, ultimately, rendered pointless by the fact that most of the time, the customer would immediately dump everything in the bowl themselves. Observing this habit told me that these folks had only listened to half of the reasoning behind that whole "on the side" thing.

In this chapter, though, I'm not focusing on low-cal, mixed green options - I'm looking at ways to maximize your dollar and flavor. On that topic I'll say only this - if you want a nice salad with minimal calories, put a bunch of mixed greens in a bowl. Add chopped, raw or steamed and chilled vegetables that you like. Most vegetables (except potatoes and sweet corn and their ilk) have either zero calories or a negligible calorie count. Olive oil has about 110 calories per tablespoon, and balsamic vinegar has about 15 calories per tablespoon. Add all the herbs you want, add some olive oil and vinegar. Sprinkle on some salt and pepper. Boom! Enjoy your relatively low-cal salad. Now that we've moved past that, let's get into other kinds of salad that are far more interesting! And if you're feeling really motivated to do so, just put these on a bed of greens. You won't regret it.

Remember, fresh herbs are an
easy way to make salad interesting.
Just add them to your lettuce mix.
Don't tell anyone.
Just let everyone think you're a wizard.

Bacon & Bleu Potato Salad

Again, we aren't looking at healthy, so much, as we ARE looking at delicious. This is a magnificent side to bring to any summer barbeque. And, like so many recipes in here, feel free to modify to meet your tastes.

What You Need:
3 lbs Russet Potatoes
1 medium red onion, minced fine
2 ribs of celery, minced fine
6 slices of bacon
½ Cup Blue Cheese Crumbles
1 Cup Mayonnaise
½ Cup Sour Cream
¼ Cup White Wine Vinegar
2 Tablespoons Garlic, minced
2 Tablespoons + 1 Teaspoon kosher salt
1 Teaspoon Coarse Ground pepper *(or ½ teaspoon fine ground)*
2 Green Onions, chopped for garnish

Preheat your oven to 375 degrees.

Scrub your potatoes clean, and cut into 1" cubes. No need to peel them! Put these in a large cooking pot with enough water to cover, with 2 Tablespoons of Kosher Salt. Bring just to a boil, and reduce heat to medium simmer. Let the potatoes cook until you can slip a knife into a piece of the potato with little or no effort.

While your potatoes are simmering, bake your bacon until it's crisped - around 30 minutes.

Once your potatoes are cooked, dump them into a colander, and let them drain. Move them into a large mixing bowl to cool.

When your bacon is well cooked, transfer to a paper towel-lined plate to absorb the excess grease.

Now, to the dressing. In a smaller mixing bowl, combine your mayonnaise, sour cream, vinegar, onion, celery, garlic, salt and pepper. Mix thoroughly. Fold in half of the blue cheese crumbles. After your potatoes are cooled to room temperature, move them to a larger mixing bowl, then pour your dressing mixture over your potatoes, and gently fold the dressing through the potatoes, taking care to not crush the potatoes too much.

Crumble in your bacon and remaining blue cheese and fold into the mixture. Refrigerate for an hour or two, at least. Garnish with your green onions before serving.

Sort Of A Tabbouleh Salad

While bulgur wheat is traditional, you can also do this with couscous, quinoa or even orzo. This isn't exactly an authentic traditional Levantine recipe, but it's one I make a lot in the warmer months. If you're lucky enough to have a garden, or space for herb pots at home, grow mint and flat leaf parsley to keep you in good supply all summer. They're the easiest herbs in the world to grow.

What You Need:
1 Cup Bulgur Wheat
2 Cups Italian (Flat Leaf) Parsley, chopped fine
½ Cup Mint Leaves, chopped fine
1 Can Garbanzo Beans *(Regular size, 12-14 oz.)*
1 Cup Roma Tomatoes *(chopped into approximately ½" dice)*
1 Cup Black or Kalamata Olives, sliced or chopped
1 Cup Cucumber *(chopped into approximately ½" dice)*
½ Cup Green Onions, chopped
½ Cup Radish, thinly sliced or cut into matchsticks

Dressing
½ Cup Vinegar *(White wine or Champagne Vinegar is a great option here!)*
½ Cup Olive Oil
¼ Cup Lemon Juice
1 Tablespoon minced garlic
1 Teaspoon salt
½ Teaspoon black pepper

Optional, but delicious to add to the dressing:
¼ Teaspoon Allspice
¼ Teaspoon Cinnamon

Start by soaking your bulgur wheat in 2 cups of boiling water. Leave it to soak, off the heat, for 30 minutes. Stir it every 10 minutes or so while it's soaking. If there's still water after 30 minutes, let it continue to soak until most is absorbed. If it's softened enough to eat without it being unpleasant, and there's still water, drain off the excess. Set aside to cool.

Prepare your vegetables and herbs, and fold them together in a large mixing bowl. Add your bulgur wheat.

Whisk together your dressing, and pour across the contents of your mixing bowl. Thoroughly mix together, and refrigerate for an hour or so before serving. Mix again before serving. Sprinkle with goat cheese or feta crumbles. Offer your guests floss for the green herbs that will definitely be caught in their teeth.

Garbage Pasta Salad

This is one of those "Let's use up the leftovers!" recipes that I absolutely adore. It's definitely a recipe that will change every time you make it, depending on what you have in the refrigerator at the time. It's also an opportunity to use up little bits of leftover pasta you have around - a mix of rotini, penne and other short pastas always make for an interesting side dish. I've DEFINITELY put chopped grilled chicken into it for a delicious and easy lunch. This recipe is just a starting place - once you have the hang of it, improvise with it. If there IS a "secret" to it, for me, it's to have a good balance of pickled vegetables, chopped fresh vegetables, some sort of bean, some sort of cheese and if you like, some sort of meat - salami, pepperoni, chicken, etc.

What You Need:
2 cups dry rotini or penne
1 can artichoke hearts (14-16 oz), roughly chopped
1 can garbanzo beans
1 cup broccoli and/or cauliflower (cut into small florets)
1 cup mozzarella or pepperjack cheese (cut into ½ inch cubes)
1 cup chopped salami or pepperoni
½ cup sliced black olives
½ cup finely chopped red onion or shallot
½ cup chopped pickled sweet peppers or pepperoncini rings

Dressing:
1 cup olive oil (the greenest you can get!)
½ cup vinegar (any vinegar is great, I like balsamic or champagne vinegar)
1 Tablespoon dry Italian Herb Mix
½ Teaspoon ground black pepper
¼ Teaspoon salt (adjust to your taste)

Start by cooking your pasta, JUST to the point that it's cooked. Remove from heat, pour into a colander and rinse with cool water to stop the cooking. Shake out the cool water, and let it drain for a few moments.

Mix up the dressing ingredients - whisk together, or shake in a jar.

Add the vegetables, cheese and meat to the pasta, and toss together. Shake your dressing again, and pour it evenly over the mixture, and fold it all together. Refrigerate for an hour, and mix again. Before you serve it, mix it together again to re-distribute the dressing.

This keeps nicely for a few days in the refrigerator, and makes an excellent go-to lunch or midnight snack. Serve over salad greens if you're feeling super fancy.

Sweet & Sour Coleslaw

If you aren't a fan of cole slaw because you've only ever had that mayonnaise-based, weirdly sweet variety from the grocery store and fast food places, this might be an option that would convert you. I always like a little bit of spice in my coleslaw, and this is definitely one that can bring some heat. You can use pretty much any sort of cabbage here - I like this one with napa cabbage, but sometimes it's hard to find. A mix of purple and white is always visually nice, but pre-bagged white cabbage is perfectly fine for this recipe.

What You Need:
6 Cups shredded cabbage
1 Cup shredded carrots
1 Cup finely chopped onion
1 Cup finely sliced red bell pepper
1 Cup jicama, cut into matchsticks

Dressing:
1 Cup apple cider or rice wine vinegar
¼ Cup vegetable oil
2 Tablespoons of brown sugar
1 Tablespoon brown mustard
1 Tablespoon celery seed
1 teaspoon Chinese five spice
1 teaspoon kosher salt *(or ½ teaspoon table salt)*
¼ teaspoon chili powder

Start by prepping your vegetables, and folding them together, so everything is evenly distributed.

In a medium sized mixing bowl, whisk the dressing ingredients together. Pour across the vegetable mix, until everything is well coated. Toss veggies and dressing by hand. Cover your mixture, and refrigerate for an hour. Remove from refrigeration, and mix everything together again, and return to the refrigerator. Repeat this refrigerate and stir cycle, every 30-45 minutes for at LEAST 4 hours before you serve. If you're able to let the mixture refrigerate overnight, so much the better. It's actually a mixture that seems to get better when it marinates longer.

Coronation Chicken Salad

Probably my favorite cold sandwich salad! This is based on a recipe by chef Rosemary Hume in 1953, originally made for the coronation lunch of Queen Elizabeth II. One food historian records it as a nod to the Jubilee Chicken dish that was prepared for George V's Silver Jubilee celebration in 1935. That original recipe was modified, and was geared toward using ingredients that would have been available in a post-war England. Rationing was nearing its end in 1953, but there would have still been shortages of some ingredients so this was a simplified lunch recipe that nearly anyone could have made. Today, though, this adaptation has quickly become another of my favorites that involve using up leftover chicken.

What You Need:

4 Cups chopped chicken (leftover, cold, off the bone)
½ Cup finely chopped onion
½ Cup finely chopped celery
½ Cup finely chopped parsley

Dressing:

¾ Cup mayonnaise
½ Cup sour cream or crème fraîche
¼ cup mild curry powder
2 Tablespoons apricot jam or preserves
1 Tablespoon tomato paste
1 teaspoon mild chili powder (or hotter if you like the heat!)
¼ teaspoon ground black pepper
Salt, to taste

Combine your chicken, onion, celery and parsley.

In a separate bowl, whisk together the mayonnaise, sour cream, apricot jam and tomato paste until it's well combined. Whisk in curry powder, chili powder and black pepper. Once it's mixed, pour over the chicken and vegetable mixture and fold together. Transfer to a covered dish or plastic container and refrigerate for at least an hour before serving. Leftovers keep nicely, refrigerated, for up to three days. But honestly, I've never had leftovers that long.

Serve on buttered toast as sandwiches, or as a spread with crackers.

Panzanella

This is literally a salad with bread as the main ingredient. Carb lovers rejoice! Generally speaking, I wouldn't use leftover sliced sandwich bread for this one, it's more for the leftover French boule, baguette or Italian loaf from the bakery. While they are delicious, and I do love those, they don't tend to be fresh for more than a day or two, and are perfect in this recipe. Now, we're looking for slightly stale bread, here, but not rock hard.

What You Need:
¼ Cup olive oil, or non-stick pan spray
4 Cups stale bread, cut into 1" cubes
3 Cups diced tomatoes, or cherry tomatoes, sliced in half vertically
2 Cups English cucumber, sliced slightly thick, and cut into half-moons
1 Cup bell pepper, chopped into ½" pieces (any color is great!)
1 Cup, roughly chopped basil
½ Cup goat cheese crumbles
½ Cup red onion, cut into thin strips
¼ Cup capers, drained *(optional, but a tasty addition!)*

Dressing:
½ cup olive oil
½ cup vinegar *(white wine, or champagne vinegar are also delicious here!)*
1 Tablespoon Dijon mustard
1 Teaspoon salt
½ Teaspoon pepper

Preheat your oven to 325 degrees. On a cookie sheet, spread out your stale bread. Sprinkle with olive oil, and a little kosher salt. Bake for about 15 minutes, or until the bread is crunchy. Remove from the oven, and let it cool.

In a large mixing bowl, combine your chopped vegetables, goat cheese and basil. Add your cooled bread.

In a smaller mixing bowl, whisk together your dressing until smooth and well combined. Pour evenly over the bread and vegetable mixture. Toss mixture until it's well combined. Let the mixture rest for about 30 minutes, then mix again to combine flavors before serving. And yes, you can serve it over a bed of salad greens, or incorporate cold leftover chicken.

Thunder & Lightning

Truthfully, this is barely a salad and barely a recipe. My understanding of this "salad" came from the rush to pick the VERY ripe cucumbers and tomatoes in the garden when a summer thunderstorm was coming. Heavy winds and rain meant that they'd likely be ripped from the vine and destroyed. And it would be very easy to preserve them in vinegar for a few days, and be able to enjoy the bounty of your garden. For some reason, this is a favorite among guests who come to my house in the summer. It's annoyingly simple.

What You Need:
2 Cucumbers
3 Medium Tomatoes
2 Medium Onions

Dressing:
2 Cups Vinegar (white, or apple cider, depending on what you like)
1 Tablespoon Salt
1 Teaspoon Sugar
¼ teaspoon ground black pepper
Pinch of chili powder, adjust to taste

Slice your onion, cucumber and tomato into thin slices and gently layer them together in a large mixing bowl.

In a separate mixing bowl, combine the vinegar, salt, sugar, chili and pepper. Pour the dressing mixture over the vegetables. Gently swirl in the bowl until everything is covered, and seasoning is evenly distributed throughout. Leave marinating in the refrigerator for at least 2 hours before serving. It keeps fabulously in the refrigerator for a week or so.

> **PRO TIP:** *I have kept a bowl of this going for weeks in the refrigerator by adding more vegetables to the mix, as I've served out part of it... a couple cups of veggies out, add a couple back in. It's the perpetual salad. Replace the vinegar mixture as it gets low.*

- CHAPTER 9 -
Side Dishes

Much like appetizers, side dishes are frequently the stars of the dinner show. I mean, how often do we swap recipes for the turkey after Thanksgiving? Not very often. It's always your friend's weird version of the green bean casserole or corn pudding that you want to know more about or it's a particularly delicious take on mashed potatoes that elevate everything around it.

Of course, it's easy to adapt many of these into entrees. We too frequently assume that the "main" dish has to be some kind of meat, or particularly protein heavy. This is not always the case. Look to these recipes as a jump-off point for any number of adaptations.

Macaroni & Cheese

This is definitely one that can be adapted to a main dish SO easily. This recipe is the base recipe, and there are endless options for things you can add in - bacon, taco-seasoned ground turkey, stewed beef, roasted chicken... if you like meat. But also, pretty much any vegetable that you like - truly, it can make vegetables you don't like infinitely better. When you're adding meat, make sure it's cooked before you mix it in. And depending on the vegetable, you may want to steam it before you bake it in - dense vegetables like cauliflower, carrots, potatoes, etc. won't cook all the way through when they're mixed into this macaroni and cheese recipe. Note, this recipe can become a little expensive considering all of the cheese that's involved, but it's probably not something you'll be making all the time. It's VERY worth it when you do.

What You Need:
Béchamel Sauce (see chapter 5)
1 cup whole milk
½ cup fine minced green onion
1 lb.. Elbow Macaroni (substitute with rigatoni or penne, if you prefer)
2 cups shredded cheddar cheese
1 cup shredded mozzarella or Monterey Jack cheese
1 cup shredded smoked gouda
1 cup shredded or chopped swiss or emmental cheese
½ cup shredded parmesan
½ cup breadcrumbs or panko
¼ cup water

Preheat your oven to 350 degrees.

In a large pot, bring water to a boil, and simmer your pasta until it's a firm al dente - usually this takes about 5 minutes of low simmering. Once it's ready, pour it into a colander and shake out as much water as you can. Transfer the pasta to a large mixing bowl.

In the pan with your prepared béchamel, add your cup of milk, green onions, and your shredded cheeses. Gently mix until your cheeses are melted. Pour this mixture over the pasta in the mixing bowl and fold everything together. Add ¼ cup of water to the mixture, and pour into a buttered roasting pan. Sprinkle the breadcrumbs and parmesan across the top.

Loosely lay foil across the top of the pan, and bake for 15 minutes. Remove the foil, rotate the pan and bake for another 15-20 minutes, or until the top of the pan is browned to your liking. Finished cooking temperature should be 160 degrees in the middle of the pan.

Let it rest for 5-10 minutes before serving.

Corn Pudding

This is truly a Thanksgiving favorite that everyone loves, and I am loath to admit how truly, ridiculously simple it actually is. Foolishly, I tend to forget that it can be made any time, not just Thanksgiving, and I always lament that I could have this, literally, any time. It's also NOT a low calorie dish, and frankly I'm not sure I'd be interested in a "diet" version. It's the richness of the dish, and the fact that it's not something you have every day that makes it so marvelous.

What You Need:

3 Tablespoons butter
¼ cup breadcrumbs
1 box Jiffy® Corn Muffin Mix *(Prepared according to box directions)*
1 can creamed corn *(14 oz - ish)*
2 cups frozen sweet corn *(not in a sauce!)*
1 cup shredded cheddar cheese *(Set aside ¼ cup of the cheddar for topping)*
½ cup sour cream
1 small can (2-4 oz) chopped, mild green chilis, well drained

Preheat your oven to 375 degrees. Butter a souffle dish, or smaller baking dish, then coat the buttered surface with your breadcrumbs..

Mix your Jiffy® Corn Muffin mix according to the directions on the box. To this muffin mix, add your can of creamed corn and frozen corn. Stir in the sour cream and fold in the cheese. Fold in your green chilis.

Pour mixture into the baking dish, sprinkle the top with ¼ cup of shredded cheddar. Bake for approximately 45 minutes, or until the sides are brown, and the top springs back with little pressure. Insert a toothpick into the center - if it comes back MOSTLY clean, it's done. If it's still a little moist, that's okay. If it comes back coated with batter, put it back in the oven for an additional 5 minutes at a time, until it's done.

Pomme Dauphinoise

You already know this as "potatoes au gratin", but this Frenchest of French dishes is TRULY magnificent to present on a table. Like so many southern French dishes, it involves very few ingredients, but the technique is everything - evenly, thinly, sliced potatoes are easy to achieve with a mandoline, but a slow, steady knife can also achieve perfect cuts. Adding fresh or dried herbs to the milk mixture adds some deliciousness, too, but is definitely less French than the original. Gruyère, by the way, tends to be a little more expensive than Swiss, Mozzarella or a cheddar, so feel free to substitute as you see fit.

What You Need:
2 lbs russet potatoes, peeled
2 cups grated Gruyère
1 ¾ cups whole milk
3 cloves garlic, finely minced
4 tablespoons unsalted butter
2 teaspoon kosher salt

Preheat your oven to 450 degrees, and butter a 9x12 baking dish.

In a medium sized saucepan, heat your milk, minced garlic and salt. Stir slowly until small bubbles start to form on the perimeter of the pan. Remove from the heat. Let it cool on the stovetop.

Somewhat thinly (¼", or thereabouts) slice your potatoes. Lay them out flat on a tea towel to help remove excess moisture. Separate the potatoes into thirds.

Layer one third of the potatoes into the bottom of a buttered baking dish, tiling the potato slices, slightly overlapping, until the bottom of the pan is well covered. Sprinkle a third of the Gruyère across the top of the potato layer. Add the next third of the potato slices in an even layer, add the next third of the cheese across the top. Repeat one last time - layer of potatoes, layer of cheese.

Stir your milk & garlic mixture, and pour slowly over the pan of potatoes and cheese. Grind a little black pepper over the top of the pan. Bake for approximately 30 minutes, or until the top is well browned. Remove from the oven, and let rest for 5-10 minutes until the bubbling slows, and the cheese thickens a bit.

If, for some reason, you do have leftovers at the end of dinner, this keeps beautifully for 2-3 days. Or freeze single servings for quick dinners.

Vegetable Napoleon

Napoleons are traditionally a type of dessert, but it really just refers to the stacking of delicious things. I will admit that this is a bit of a detail heavy, fiddly dish to make - there's a lot of parts - and it takes some time. BUT it really is worth it in the end. This recipe will make six servings, but can be scaled infinitely. This is also an easy one to adapt to a fully vegan version.

What You Need:
2 medium, russet potatoes
6 Portobello Mushrooms (3-4" in diameter)
6 slices of smoked gouda
1 large, or two smaller red bell peppers
3 small-ish zucchinis (7-8" length)
1 can diced tomatoes (14-16 oz)
1 cup breadcrumbs or panko
½ cup vegetable oil
2 eggs
¼ cup flour
2 Tablespoons Worcestershire sauce, or liquid amino acids
1 Tablespoon minced garlic
1 teaspoon fennel seed
½ cup minced parsley
¼ cup shredded parmesan
Black Pepper
Kosher Salt
6 skewers

Preheat your oven to 400 degrees.

Let's start with the potatoes. Grate the potatoes - skin on. Put the grated potatoes in a bowl of iced water, and a tablespoon of kosher salt. Swirl the potato shreds in the water, and let it rest for 15 minutes, or so. This will help pull out the excess starch from the potatoes.

While the potatoes are soaking, pop the stems off the portobello mushrooms. Brush any excess dirt from the surface of the mushrooms, and slice the mushroom cap cross-wise, like a hamburger bun, so you're left with two mushroom slices from each. Arrange the mushroom slices on a plate (or two) and sprinkle with Worcestershire sauce. They don't need to be soaked in it, just a couple tablespoons for all of them. Leave the mushrooms to absorb the sauce.

Cut the stem and blossom end off the zucchini. Slice your zucchini lengthwise - to get four slices. Cut those in half, across, so you're left with 8 slices of zucchini that are about 3-4 inches long. Repeat with the other two zucchini. You should have 24 slices of zucchini.

Cut the stem off of your bell pepper(s). Rub the outside of your pepper with olive oil, sprinkle with salt, and set them on a sheet pan. Put them in the oven - top rack - for about 15 minutes, or until they're softened. Remove from the oven, and drop them into a plastic container, and place the lid on. The steaming will help make the skin easy to remove. After about 10 minutes, remove them from the container, peel off as much of the skin as you can, and slice into ½" strips.

In a small saucepan, heat your tomatoes over a low heat. Add the garlic and fennel seeds, a teaspoon of salt and the black pepper. Once the tomatoes start to bubble, stir gently, put on the lid, and turn off the heat. Let the mixture rest and cool.

Now, back to the potatoes. Pour your soaking potatoes into a mesh sieve, and drain off the water. As much as possible, wring out the water from the potatoes - if needs be, roll them in a tea towel and twist the excess water out. In a mixing bowl, blend the eggs, flour, a teaspoon of salt, and ¼ teaspoon of black pepper. Mix in the potatoes. Form the potatoes into fairly thin patties (½" or so), and dredge them into the breadcrumbs. Fry the potatoes in a saute pan with oil, or deep fry them until they're golden brown. You'll want to make 12. Remove them to a paper towel-lined plate.

Now, let's assemble the stacks! On a baking sheet, lined with foil or parchment, lay out six of your potato cakes. Next, add a slice of portobello mushroom. Then criss-cross two slices of zucchini. Spoon a tablespoon or two of the tomato mixture on top of the zucchini. Add another slice of portobello mushroom, lay a couple strips of the bell pepper across the mushroom, spoon on a bit more of the tomato mixture, lay on a slice of cheese, add a couple strips of the bell pepper, and put another potato cake on top. Insert a skewer into each stack to hold them together.

Once you've got all your stacks made, gently move them into the oven. Bake at 400 degrees for 10 minutes. Reduce the heat to 350, and bake an additional 10-15 minutes, or until the mushrooms have softened, and the cheese has melted.

When you remove them from the oven, gently set the pan on a rack to cool for about 10 minutes. Carefully remove each, with the skewer still inserted, onto the plate you're serving from. Remove the skewers once you're ready to serve.

Sprinkle with chopped parsley and parmesan cheese.

Ratatouille

If you can't tell by what you've read so far in this book, I have a DEEP love, and admiration for country French cookery. As with much of Provençal cuisine, it's all about fresh, flavorful ingredients, and letting them do their own thing, without dressing them up with a lot of excess saucing, or overworking. This recipe isn't entirely traditional - although there isn't a singular consensus on what IS a completely, authentically Provençal Ratatouille. What I can tell you, is that it's absolutely delicious alongside roast meat of pretty much any sort.

What You Need:
2 Small Eggplants (Japanese variety is perfect here!)
2 Zucchini (smallish - 7-8")
2 Yellow Summer Squash
1 Yellow onion, chopped fine
1 Red Bell Pepper
2 Tablespoons minced garlic
1 large can of crushed tomatoes (approximately 28 oz)
2 Tablespoons of fresh thyme leaves
½ cup chopped basil leaves
½ cup fine minced parsley
¼ cup olive oil

Preheat your oven to 350 degrees.

Start by slicing your eggplant, zucchini and squash into circles, about ½" thick. Sprinkle with salt, and pepper, and set aside. Slice the yellow bell pepper into strips.

In a large saucepan, add your olive oil. Heat the oil, onion, garlic and thyme leaves until the garlic and onion start to sizzle and become slightly translucent. Add your tomatoes, and heat until the tomatoes start to bubble. Stir, and turn off the heat.

In a baking dish/casserole dish, spoon in about half of the tomato sauce. On top, layer the zucchini, eggplant and yellow squash, alternating between them - overlapping until all have been layered into the dish. Layer in the yellow pepper strips, and pour over the remaining tomato sauce. Cover your baking dish, loosely, with foil.

Bake for 20 minutes, and remove the foil. Return to the oven for 10 minutes more, or until the tomato sauce is bubbling. Remove from the oven, sprinkle the minced parsley and basil across the top, and allow to cool for about 10 minutes.

This dish is also delicious cold for summer lunches on the patio.

Glazed Chickpeas & Carrots

Okay, I know this might sound like a weird combination, but it's absolutely delicious. This is definitely one of those recipes you can really play with, and adjust flavors to your personal taste. It's also one that's really fun to make super spicy! The sweetness of the carrots and nuttiness of the chickpeas make for a nearly endless list of flavor options - make them sweet, make them herbaceous, make them hot, hot, HOT if you want. This recipe is a spicy-sweet version that isn't TOO hot... but if you want to bring the heat, just amp up the chili powder and the ginger.

What You Need:

6 Carrots, peeled, and cut into ½" thick coins
1 can Chickpeas/Garbanzo Beans
2 tablespoons olive oil
¼ cup butter (½ stick)
2 Tablespoons dark brown sugar
1 teaspoon cumin
1 teaspoon garlic powder
½ teaspoon chili powder
½ teaspoon ground ginger
¼ teaspoon cinnamon

Put a saucepan with a quart of water over medium heat on the stovetop. Add your carrot slices to the water, and simmer on medium heat for about 5 minutes.

In a small mixing bowl, mix together the brown sugar, cumin, garlic powder, chili powder, ginger and cinnamon.

While your carrots are simmering, drain the liquid off of the chickpeas, and rinse them with cool water. Dump them into a saute pan on medium heat, with two tablespoons of olive oil and a sprinkling of salt. Toss the chickpeas around in the pan until it's well coated with oil, and the chickpeas start to toast and brown. Reduce the heat to low, add the butter until it's mostly melted, and add the carrots. Stir gently to coat everything with the butter.

Sprinkle the sugar and spice mixture over the carrots and chickpeas. Stir gently until everything is coated, and the sugar has melted into the butter. Keep the heat as low as possible - watch it closely - if things look like they're starting to get too dark, remove from the heat. Once everything is coated, let it simmer on a very low heat until the carrots have softened as much as you like. Remove from the heat, and transfer to a serving bowl. Cover and allow to rest for at least 5 minutes before serving.

Delicious over basmati rice, on its own, or with roasted chicken or lamb.

Roasted Brussels Sprouts

I'm always fascinated when vegetables find themselves "on trend" or suddenly very popular due to the culinary geniuses on social media platforms who "discover" recipes that are actually just the way that poor people have prepared them for ages. Is there a term for that? Culinary Christopher Columbus-ing, perhaps? Brussels Sprouts are polarizing, for sure - like most members of genus brassicae, they have a sulphurous taste that cooking mostly removes, But the residual taste can put some people off. Brussels sprouts benefit from fast, high heat, and strong seasoning. This recipe is a deep simplification. Season and garnish as you wish.

What You Need:

2 lbs. Brussels Sprouts
½ cup grated parmesan cheese
¼ cup olive oil
½ teaspoon kosher salt
½ teaspoon sugar (optional, but delicious!)
¼ teaspoon black pepper

Preheat your oven to 450 degrees.

Cut your brussels sprouts vertically through the base and up through the top into halves. Toss the sprouts with olive oil, sugar, salt and pepper until well coated. Arrange the sprouts on a baking sheet with the cut sides down. Roast for 25 minutes, or until you can easily sink a fork into the sprouts.

Sprinkle with parmesan before serving.

Creamed Spinach

It's the rare restaurant that still bothers to put this old geezer of a recipe on their menus. But it's such a favorite, and so easy to make, that it would be a shame to not include it here. Feel free to make this recipe with kale, instead of spinach, if you're into that sort of thing. I use frozen spinach here, but if you have fresh, just chop it down and blanch it for about 20 seconds before the sauteing part of the recipe.

What You Need:

1 shallot, or small onion, minced fine
2 packages of frozen spinach (approximately 20-24 oz total.), thawed
½ cup cream cheese
½ cup mozzarella
½ cup parmesan cheese
2 tablespoons minced garlic cloves
2 tablespoons butter
¼ teaspoon black pepper

In a mixing bowl, leave your cream cheese to soften.

In a large saute pan over medium heat, melt your butter, and heat your shallot or onion until it starts to become translucent. Add your garlic. Mix together, and add your spinach.

Once your spinach is heated through, add your cream cheese. Melt the cream cheese through your spinach mixture, and add your parmesan cheese and pepper. Mix everything together and cook until it bubbles slightly around the edges and the mixture thickens slightly. Remove from heat and serve.

Sweet Potato & Blue Cheese Tarts

You can certainly make these in tart pans, but if you only have a muffin tin available, that will work perfectly well. These savory-sweet tarts are also delicious cold, from the refrigerator. Indeed, these are perfect for a late night snack. This recipe does involve a number of steps, but it isn't particularly difficult, I promise.

What You Need:

The Pastry
2 Cups Flour
½ Cup Butter (1 stick)
1 cup very cold water

The Filling
3 Sweet Potatoes
2 Yellow Onions
½ Cup Blue Cheese Crumbles, plus an additional 2 Tablespoons for garnish
2 Tablespoons butter
2 Tablespoon olive oil
¼ cup cream cheese
1 Tablespoon dried sage

The Garnish
3 Green Onions, minced

Preheat your oven to 400 degrees.

Scrub your potatoes clean, and coat with olive oil. Wrap your potatoes in foil with an ice cube, and a teaspoon of salt sprinkled over the potatoes. Bake for 45-50 minutes, or until you can poke them through with a fork.

While your potatoes are baking, slice your onions thinly, and begin sauteing them in a tablespoon of olive oil and 2 Tablespoons of butter in a shallow saute pan or skillet. Sprinkle with salt and a little pepper. Cook until they start to darken. Reduce the heat to very low, and let them caramelize further. When they've darkened to a nice deep golden color, remove them from the heat, and transfer them to a small mixing bowl to cool.

Now, start your pastry. Cut your butter into small pieces, and add to the butter. Blend the flour and butter in your food processor. And blend until the flour mixture appears crumbly, and starts to stick together. Dump into a mixing bowl, and add your cold water bit by bit until it comes together in a dough. Once it's a solid dough, knead it together for a minute, wrap in plastic, and refrigerate.

Start mashing your cream cheese, blue cheese and sage in a separate bowl. Let it soften a bit while you're waiting for the potatoes to finish baking.

When the timer on your potatoes goes off, remove them from the oven. Test with a toothpick. Once you can easily sink a toothpick into your potatoes, they're ready. If they need more time, return them to the oven, 10 minutes at a time, until they're softened adequately. Reduce your oven's heat to 350.

Once they're cool enough to handle, scrape the filling out of the potatoes, and add the filling to the cheese mixture. Fold them into the cheese, and mix until the sweet potatoes and cheese are smoothly blended. Let it rest.

Pull out your muffin tin, or tart pans and butter them liberally - or use non-stick pan spray. Take your pastry from the refrigerator, and knead it lightly until you shape it into a rectangle. Cut the rectangle into 12 equal pieces. Roll each piece into a circle, and fit them into the muffin tins or tart pans. Score the bottom of each pastry with a few pokes of a fork. Partially bake your empty pastry shells for 10 minutes. Remove the pastries from the oven.

In the bottom of the pastry shells, spoon in about a tablespoon of the caramelized onion mixture. On top, spoon in the sweet potato and cheese mixture. Fill to the top, and smooth out the top. Sprinkle some blue cheese crumbles on top. Return your filled pastries to the oven for 15 minutes.

Allow to cool, remove from the pan and serve. Garnish with chopped green onion.

Cold Sesame Noodles

I suppose this could be considered a salad, but since the noodles are the real star of the show here, I'm not so sure. I've easily made an entire meal out of this, but it also goes nicely as a side to sushi. You can certainly use any sort of noodles you like - udon, vermicelli, etc. but I like the soba noodles for this one, because of the rich, nutty flavor. It goes so nicely with the green onion and sesame flavors.

What You Need:
2 Cups chopped, cold chicken (optional, but mighty tasty)
1 lb. soba noodles
2 cups green beans (fresh or frozen)
1 cup green onion, chopped fine
½ cup soy sauce or tamari
¼ cup rice wine vinegar
¼ cup sesame oil
1 Tablespoon of sugar
1 Tablespoon sesame seeds
1 teaspoon black pepper

Start a large pot of water on your stove at high heat.

While your water is heating, whisk together your soy sauce, rice wine vinegar, sesame oil, sugar and black pepper.

Once your water is boiling, add your noodles. Stir your noodles until they just start to soften. Reduce the heat to medium. Add your green beans. Allow to simmer for about 6 minutes and remove from the heat. Let your noodles and green beans sit for another minute off the heat, and dump into a colander. Rinse with cold water, and drain off the excess water.

In a large mixing bowl, add your noodles and green beans. Pour over your dressing mixture, and toss the noodles in the dressing. Add your chicken, green onion and sesame seeds. Lightly toss those together and refrigerate for at least 30 minutes before serving.

PRO-TIP: *I have DEFINITELY used bottled salad dressing for this one when I was short on time or ingredients, instead of making it from scratch. Pretty much every grocery store will carry some sort of Sesame-Soy dressing. No one needs to know!*

Glazed & Spiced Roasted Vegetables

You can truly use any number of vegetables you like in this dish, but for this recipe I've included the ones that I love, and tend to be the most available. But when they're available, consider parsnips, turnips, rutabagas, and firm winter squashes.

What You Need:

3 cups carrot, roughly chopped (approximately ½" thick coins)
3 cups cauliflower, cut into florets
3 cups sweet potato, cut into 1" chunks
2 cups red onion, cut into 1" chunks
2 cups green or yellow bell pepper, cut into 1" pieces
½ cup vegetable oil
¼ cup vinegar (apple cider, or white wine are delicious here!)
1 tablespoon brown sugar
2 teaspoons garlic powder
2 teaspoons cumin
1 teaspoon kosher salt
½ teaspoon black pepper
½ teaspoon cinnamon

Garnish:

½ cup finely chopped parsley for garnish
1 tablespoon of lemon zest, and ¼ cup of lemon juice

Preheat the oven to 450 degrees.

Start by cutting your vegetables into bite-sized chunks - about 1". In a large pot, start simmering 2 quarts of water, with a tablespoon of salt. Once your water starts to boil, reduce it to a simmer, and drop your vegetables into the water. Let them simmer for 1 minute, then remove them - straining off the water - to a large mixing bowl. Let them rest.

In a separate, smaller mixing bowl, combine the oil, vinegar, brown sugar, the salt and spices. Whisk together until the mixture resembles a thick slurry. Make sure there are no lumps of sugar. Pour the mixture over the vegetables, and mix it throughout, coating all of the vegetables. Pour the mixture into a large roasting pan, and spread it evenly.

Bake it at 450 degrees for 15 minutes. Remove the pan from the oven, and mix and turn the vegetables around in the pan, re-coating them with the seasoning mixture. Reduce the oven heat to 350, and continue to bake for an additional 15 minutes. Once they've browned, and the carrots have softened, it should be ready to eat.

Remove from the oven, and transfer to the serving dish. Garnish with the parsley, lemon juice and lemon zest.

Salt Roasted Potatoes

This is another ridiculously easy recipe and it's always a crowd pleaser. Chili powder is also a nice addition to the finished seasoning if you're looking for a spicier version.

What You Need:

12 Small red or white potatoes
½ cup finely chopped onion
4 cloves of garlic, finely chopped.
½ cup olive oil, approximately
½ cup finely chopped fresh dill
Kosher salt
Black pepper

Preheat your oven to 375 degrees.

In a large cooking pot, add the potatoes, onions, garlic and enough water to cover. Bring to near a boil, and reduce the heat and simmer everything for 7 minutes. Drain the potatoes, onions and garlic into a fine sieve and transfer to a roasting pan that you've oiled with half of the olive oil. Once the potato mixture is in the pan, drizzle and coat with the rest of the olive oil.

Sprinkle with a teaspoon or so of kosher salt. Roast for about 10 minutes. Test for doneness - if a knife easily slips into the potato, it's done. If not, return to the oven for 5 minutes at a time until they're done.

Remove from the oven, and gently stir around the pan, sprinkle with another teaspoon of kosher salt and chopped dill. Let them rest for 5 minutes or so before serving.

Serve hot, with sour cream on the side.

- CHAPTER 10 -

Main Dishes

Ah, the Main Dish. In much of western cuisine - at least English, and by extension, French traditions - this involves the primary protein, and usually that means meat. And not just meat, but a HUGE hunk of meat. Your Sunday beef roasts, whole chickens and ducks, and sometimes filets of fish, but let's be real - in the US, we're mostly talking about land creatures.

Since the 1800's, such a premium has been placed on meat in the US, and the having of meat on your dinner table that by 2018, the average American was consuming 220 pounds of meat per year. Let that number sink in. This means about 10 ounces of meat per day, per person. That's an awful lot of meat. Needless to say, it's no surprise that there are health crises being tied to American meat consumption. From high cholesterol and heart disease, to cancers, diabetes and plain old obesity.

But, our national obsession with meat is simple - meat means money. And money means prestige. For centuries in Europe, all of the animals that wandered onto a parcel of land automatically belonged to the wealthy member of the nobility that owned the land - not the indentured servant that's actually caring for the animals. Having meat in the house was an immediate sign that you had the means to pay for the care, feeding and raising of animals. When folks moved from Europe to the "New World" they carried that belief with them.

As westward expansion of the United States stole land from indigenous people, the pioneers quickly learned about agriculture in these new spaces and what the raising of animals for food could mean when you had seemingly endless grasslands and plant life that their imported sheep, pigs, chickens and cattle could graze upon. Wild game, as far as they believed, was in infinite supply - the vast expanses of the Midwest and central regions offered bison, deer, pheasant, quail, and other small game birds. Meat, it would seem, was infinite and free for the taking. Which automatically meant getting to feel like the wealthy, landed gentry that they or their predecessors had left behind.

But in this chapter I wanted to reconsider this carnivorous assumption. Please don't misunderstand, I enjoy meat and eat far too much of it. But I also recognize that humans really don't NEED to eat as much meat as we do. There will be a number of meat-based dishes in this chapter, don't you worry - but many, dare I say most, can be adapted into meatless versions with very little change to the formulation.

Parmesan Pepper Meatballs

This is one of my mom's recipes that I've adapted for my own taste. My mom was much more modest with the spice in the meatballs, preferring to add the heat to the sauce when she made her marinara. I make mine with more heat - but, this recipe is a nice compromise between the two. If you don't want spiciness, just eliminate the crushed red peppers. Truthfully, these are delicious in gravy with potatoes - more like the Swedish Meatball type, but also fantastic with a spicy red sauce. Also, make note - this recipe makes a TON of meatballs. You can cut it in half, or do what I do - make the whole recipe, and freeze half. Just freeze them on baking sheets, then transfer to a freezer bag. If they're frozen before they go into the bag, they don't stick together as much in the bag. They'll keep in the freezer for about a year.

What You Need:
1 lb.. Ground Beef
1 lb.. Ground Italian Sausage (hot or mild, up to you!)
1 lb.. Ground Turkey
1 cup parmesan cheese
1 green bell pepper
1 white onion
2 Tablespoons minced garlic
1 Tablespoon olive oil
1 egg
½ cup breadcrumbs
1 Tablespoon fennel seeds
1 teaspoon crushed red chilis
1 teaspoon oregano
1 teaspoon dried basil
1 teaspoon kosher salt
½ teaspoon cumin
½ teaspoon black pepper

Preheat your oven to 350 degrees.

Start by putting your bell pepper (stem and seed removed) and onion into the food processor and blitz until they're very finely chopped, then pulse it three more times. It should look almost like salsa when you're done. Heat a tablespoon of olive oil in a saute pan, and dump in your onion/pepper mix. Add your garlic, fennel seeds, cumin and crushed red chilis. Saute it gently until it's just starting to brown, and the moisture is starting to cook off. Transfer to a mesh sieve, and drain off the excess moisture. Let it cool in the sieve while you mix your other ingredients.

In a large mixing bowl, add your ground beef, sausage and turkey. In a small bowl, crack your egg and scramble it slightly - add it to the meat mixture. Add the oregano, basil, salt and pepper. Start mixing it all together with your hands. Make a claw with your hand, dig into the meat, and squeeze your "claw" closed. Remove your hand. Turn your bowl ¼ turn, then repeat the claw motion until it's all well incorporated. Add your pepper and onion mixture, parmesan and breadcrumbs, and repeat the claw mixing action until everything is well mixed.

If you're grossed out by mixing meat by hand, you CAN use the dough hook on your stand mixer to achieve a similar result, but be careful not to let it mix too fast or you'll end up with heavy, dense meatballs. And no one wants that. If the mixture feels dry, or particularly dense, add a tablespoon or two of water to the mixture.

Now, form the meatballs. Use a 1 oz. ice cream scoop, or by hand, form the balls - about the size of a golf ball. Roll them between the palms of your hands to form balls - don't press too hard, as you don't want to overpack them. You'll end up with around 48 meatballs. This is where you arrange them onto baking sheets. If you're planning to freeze some, put those on a separate baking sheet, and place them in a freezer. In an hour, remove them from the baking sheet and transfer them to a freezer bag.

On the other baking sheet, place your meatballs about ½ inch apart. Bake for about 30 minutes, or until the internal temperature reaches 160 degrees Fahrenheit. If you're preparing marinara sauce for them, you can bake them for 15 minutes, then transfer them to simmering tomato sauce to cook for another 30 minutes. Either way, the internal temperature should reach 160 degrees before you serve them. Serve with grated parmesan and fresh basil.

Chicken & Dumplings

This is such a comfort food classic, that I felt like I HAD to include it here. Now, many of the versions that I see are baked, casserole-type versions. Those are delicious, but this is much more of a stewlike version. I'm partial to chicken thighs here, but if you have chicken breasts, or tenders, they're also great. You can definitely use leftover roasted chicken, here, too.

What You Need:

The Stew
2 lbs boneless chicken thighs, cut into bite sized chunks
1 cup chopped celery
1 cup finely chopped onion
1 cup diced carrots
1 cup frozen peas
2 quarts chicken stock
2 Tablespoons fresh thyme leaves (or 1 Tablespoon dried)
2 Tablespoons finely minced garlic
½ teaspoon black pepper
1 tablespoon vegetable oil
Salt to taste

The Dumplings
2 cups flour - sifted
1 ¼ teaspoon baking powder
1 teaspoon salt
2 tablespoons butter - cut into small pieces
½ cup milk

In a large stew pot, over medium heat, add your vegetable oil, celery, onion, garlic and carrots. Saute until the onions start to become slightly translucent. Add your chicken chunks, and stir. Add your thyme leaves and black pepper. Cook for about 10 minutes, or until your chicken starts to brown. Add your stock, and increase your heat to medium-high. Stir everything. While you're waiting for your stew to start simmering, let's start on your dumplings.

In your food processor, mix your flour, baking powder, salt and your butter. Blitz on high until the butter is well incorporated into the flour mixture. Transfer to a mixing bowl, and mix in your milk, a tablespoon at a time until your dough comes together in a shaggy, loose ball.

Prepare a large work surface, and flour it liberally. Turn your dumpling dough onto the floured surface and flatten it slightly - the surface should be slightly sticky, but not wet. With a well floured rolling pin, roll out the dough until it's about ½ inch thick. Now, with a pizza cutter, cut into 1 inch squares. Sprinkle more flour around the dumplings, and toss them in the flour, until they don't stick together anymore.

Back to the soup - once the broth is really simmering, reduce the heat to medi-um/low, and transfer your dumplings to the broth. Stir and separate the dump-lings. Your dumplings WILL expand by at least 2 or 3 times. Add your peas, and taste your broth. Does it need more salt? More pepper? Adjust the seasoning to your taste. Steal a dumpling from the pot and taste it to see if it's done to your liking. Let it simmer low for an additional 5-10 minutes. The broth will thicken somewhat from the flour on the dumplings.

Once they're done, remove from the heat and serve immediately.

PRO TIP: Vegan meat substitutes are plentiful. If you want to go vegan, just swap the chicken for a soy version, use vegetable stock, and milk and butter substitutes for the dumplings. It's an easy swap, and you won't com-promise on flavor.

Stuffed Peppers

This is an excellent "make in advance" recipe that I love - Have it for dinner, have some to eat later in the week, and freeze some to have in a few months down the road. This isn't a quick recipe, but not particularly difficult to make. I've written this recipe with bell peppers, but if you like a little more kick, you can use poblanos or Hungarian wax peppers.

What You Need:
½ cup rice
1 cup water
1 teaspoon salt
1 lb. ground pork
1 lb. lean ground beef (or turkey)
1 teaspoon ground cumin
1 teaspoon garlic powder
½ teaspoon chili powder
6 medium bell peppers, stems trimmed
12 slices of provolone (mozzarella, gouda, etc. are all good too!)
1 lb. rigatoni

The Sauce
1 Tablespoon of vegetable oil
2 large cans diced tomatoes
1 medium onion, minced
2 serrano chili peppers, minced (Seeds and pith removed!)
1 teaspoon salt
1 Tablespoon oregano
1 teaspoon minced fresh garlic

If you have a rice maker, drop your rice, water and salt in, and turn it on. If not, in a small saucepan, start your water on a high heat, add your rice and salt. Once it reaches boiling, reduce the heat to low. Stir your rice frequently while it's simmering. Once the water is absorbed, turn off the heat, put the lid on, and let it rest on the stove.

Preheat your own to 350 degrees.

Now, start your sauce. In a large saucepan, heat your oil, onion, garlic and serrano pepper over high heat. Saute until it's all browned, and the pepper is starting to fade to a duller green color. Sprinkle your salt and oregano, and add your tomatoes. Simmer the mixture for about 15 minutes over low heat. Remove from heat, and set aside.

In a mixing bowl, combine your pork and beef (or turkey), cumin, garlic powder, and chili powder. Add a pinch of salt and a couple pinches of black pepper. Once your rice has cooled, mix it into the meat mixture. Once the rice is evenly distributed throughout the meat mixture, refrigerate it for about 15 minutes, while you prepare your peppers.

Trim the stems on the peppers down, but don't cut it all the way off. Slice your peppers in half, vertically - scoop out the seeds and pith. Sprinkle salt inside the cavity of the peppers. With a toothpick, stab a couple holes in the sides of the pepper halves.

Scoop the filling mixture into the pepper halves, and pack in, and smooth it across the opening. Arrange them on a baking sheet (meat side up!).

Spoon a couple tablespoons of the sauce on top of the meat side of the peppers. Bake for about 30 minutes. Lay a slice of the cheese over the sauced pepper, bake for an additional 5-10 minutes. Once your cheese is melty, and slightly browned, they're ready.

While your peppers are baking, cook your rigatoni until it's just al dente. Mix the remaining sauce into the pasta. Serve your peppers on top of your pasta - garnish with chopped parsley and parmesan.

Daal With Pilau

As an adult, I've fallen more and more in love with lentils. I think a generation of sanctimonious hippies rather maligned the humble legume throughout my younger days. But since my teenage discovery of South Asian food, I came to discover a world of new options for them. Now, if you have a pressure cooker and a rice cooker, this recipe will be a snap. But even without, it's not at all difficult, and incredibly tasty.

Pilau is a fairly simple rice dish, made all over South Asia and Africa. As such, there are as many versions of it as there are people who make it. Look to this as a starting place, and adjust to your tastes.

The Daal

What You Need:
- 1 cup brown or red lentils
- 1 onion, chopped fine
- 1 teaspoon cumin seeds (or ½ teaspoon ground cumin)
- 1 teaspoon ground ginger or 1 tablespoon of grated fresh ginger
- ½ teaspoon black mustard seeds
- 2 Tablespoons ghee, or olive oil
- 2 Tablespoons of finely minced garlic
- 1 can diced tomato (approximately 12-14 ounce)
- 1 cayenne pepper, chopped - seeds and stems removed

In a large stew pot, start browning your onion in the ghee (or olive oil). Add your cumin, ginger, mustard seeds, garlic and cayenne. Saute until the onion is softened. Add your lentils, and add enough water or stock to cover your mixture by an inch. Stir, and turn your heat to high. Once it's boiling, reduce your heat to medium, and add your diced tomato. Mix, and simmer uncovered until mixture is thickened and lentils are cooked - approximately 30 minutes. The Daal will thicken as it sits.

The Pilau

What You Need:
- 1 cup Basmati Rice
- 2 cups water or vegetable stock
- 1 onion, cut into strips
- 1 cup frozen peas
- 1 Tablespoon ghee, or olive oil
- 1 teaspoon cumin seeds (or ½ teaspoon ground cumin)
- ½ teaspoon black mustard seeds
- ½ teaspoon ground turmeric
- ½ teaspoon ground coriander
- ½ teaspoon ground ginger
- 1 cinnamon stick

In a sieve, resting in a mixing bowl, start soaking your rice. Add enough water to cover your rice. Stir your rice in the water, and let the excess starch from the rice settle away from the grains of rice. Change the water 3-4 times, continuing to rinse the starch away. Once the water stays clear, your rice is ready to cook. Leave it to soak in the clear water while you prep the other ingredients.

While your rice is soaking, saute your onion, cumin and mustard seeds in the ghee or olive oil. Add a pinch of salt, and let the onions cook until they're well browned. Once they're well caramelized, remove them from the heat and let them rest.

In your rice cooker, or a large saucepan, add your 2 cups of water or stock, your soaked rice, your caramelized onions, and your spices. If you're using a saucepan, bring your mixture just to the boil, then reduce the heat to low. Stir, combining all ingredients. Let the rice simmer, uncovered. Every 10 minutes or so, stir your rice. Allow it to cook until the moisture is cooked in. This should take 20-30 minutes. Remove the cinnamon stick and fluff your rice before serving.

Spoon the Daal over the rice. Add chicken, lamb or tofu if you're so compelled, but it is absolutely delicious on its own. It keeps well in the refrigerator for up to three days. Fair warning, the spiciness will escalate the longer it stays in the fridge.

> **PRO TIP:** *Basmati rice is really the best option here. You can use jasmine or short grain white rice, but it will be much stickier, no matter how much you rinse the rice ahead of time.*

Lasagna

When it comes to advanced meal planning, there are few things that are as satisfying as a lasagna. When I was working in the 9-5 world, this was a perfect thing to make on a Sunday evening, then have a few days worth of lunches ready to go. This recipe is, also, one of the easiest to adapt to a meatless option, and if you're leaning vegan, just swap out the cheeses and meats for plant-based options. I also use egg roll wrappers instead of traditional pasta noodles, because they're a little lighter and you don't end up feeling like you've eaten a ton - but you can go with traditional pasta if you'd rather.

What You Need:

Bechamel - *see the recipe in Chapter 5*
Marinara - *also in Chapter 5*
1 lb.. package egg roll wrappers or lasagna noodles
1 lb. ground Italian sausage
1 medium onion, chopped
2 Tablespoons minced garlic
1 Tablespoon oregano
1 teaspoon fennel seeds
1 Tablespoon olive oil

¼ cup fresh basil, chopped
2 cups ricotta cheese
1 package frozen spinach - *thawed, excess water drained off*
1 egg, lightly scrambled
½ teaspoon kosher salt
¼ teaspoon black pepper
1 cup shredded mozzarella
½ cup shredded parmesan

Preheat your oven to 350 degrees, and brush olive oil inside of a 9" x 12" casserole or roasting pan. In a large saute pan, heat a tablespoon of olive oil and your onions over medium heat. As your onions start to sweat, add your garlic, fennel seeds, and the Italian sausage. Stir and cook until sausage is browned. Once your sausage is cooked, remove from the heat - drain off any excess fat that may have been released from the sausage. In a mixing bowl, combine your ricotta, spinach, egg, basil and a teaspoon of salt. Fold together.

In your baking pan, pour in ½ cup of your marinara. Spread across the bottom. Tile a single layer of your egg roll wrappers on top of the tomato sauce. Cut or tear the wrappers to fit the pan - no need to overlap them. Spoon over your ricotta and spinach mixture, and spread evenly.
Next, add another layer of egg roll wrappers, and spoon in your Italian sausage mixture. Spoon half of your marinara over the sausage mixture. Sprinkle half of your parmesan over the sausage and marinara, and top with another layer of the egg roll wrappers.
Pour over the remainder of your marinara, then pour over your bechamel. Sprinkle your mozzarella, parmesan and oregano over the top of everything.

Loosely cover your lasagna with foil, and bake for 20 minutes. It might be handy to put a cookie sheet or baking pan under the lasagna while it bakes to catch any splatter.

After 20 minutes, remove the foil from the lasagna and let it bake an additional 20-25 minutes until the top is well browned. Let it rest for 15 minutes before serving.

Meatloaf

This is one of those "mom" food staples that everyone's forgotten how to make. Or, they've had so many terrible versions that they've blocked it from their minds. I had a friend tell me that he had so much of it in school that he's never wanted to go back to it. Somehow, I don't recall ever having it as a school lunch, or even having that much of it at home, but I suspect if I had, I'd have been less compelled to revisit it. This version, however, is not the flavorless brick of those old days. I also top this with barbecue sauce. And as a native of Kansas City, I always feel the need to nod to that hometown taste.

What You Need:

- 1 lb. Ground Beef
- 1 lb. Ground Pork
- 1 lb. Ground Turkey
- 1 egg
- ½ cup breadcrumbs
- 2 Tablespoons of water
- 2 teaspoon dried oregano
- 2 teaspoon dried thyme
- 2 teaspoons garlic powder
- 1 teaspoon onion powder
- 1 teaspoon kosher salt
- ½ teaspoon black pepper
- ½ teaspoon chili powder
- ½ cup barbecue sauce

In a large mixing bowl, combine your beef, pork and turkey, then spread your meat mixture out on the bottom of the bowl. Sprinkle your breadcrumbs, your herbs and spices evenly across the meat. Lightly beat your egg, and drop it in the middle of the meat, along with the 2 Tablespoons of water. Start folding your meat over into a ball and mix it by hand until everything is well combined. Let it rest in the refrigerator for about 30 minutes. Preheat your own to 350 degrees.

Grease a loaf pan generously, and place it on a baking sheet (one with at least a ½ inch lip). Take your meatloaf from the refrigerator, and form it into a loaf and place it in your loaf pan. Move the loaf pan (on the baking sheet) into the oven. Pour one cup of hot water onto the baking sheet, so it forms a pool around the loaf pan. Bake for 20 minutes.

Remove from the oven, and pour your barbeque sauce over the top of the loaf, and spread evenly. Sprinkle a little more black pepper across the top, and return it to the oven for an additional 20 minutes. Once the center temperature reaches 165 degrees, it's done.

Remove from the oven, and let it rest for 15 minutes. Then, gently remove from the loaf pan, and place it on a platter. Moisture will be leaking, so use a platter that has a high enough edge to keep it from leaking all over the counter.

I always serve this with mashed potatoes and brown gravy. For some reason, barbeque sauce and brown gravy work really well together. True culinary alchemy.

Vegan Chili

Obviously, if you REALLY want to, you can use meat in this recipe. But I've come to love this vegan version even more. And it's delicious spooned over baked potatoes. Now, I DO add cheese and sour cream to mine, but you can always use vegan versions of those if you're so compelled. By the way, shop Latin markets for soya kernels - you can usually find it in the bulk bins, or in ½ lb.. packages for a fraction of the price at your regular supermarket. One of those packages is perfect for this recipe.

What You Need:
2 Cups dehydrated soya kernels (Texturized Vegetable Protein)
1 quart vegetable stock
1 large can diced tomatoes (approx. 28 oz.)
1 can beans, drained and rinsed (Whichever you like - black, pinto, kidney, etc.)
2 Tablespoons of vegetable oil
1 large yellow onion
1 anaheim chili
1 jalapeno
1 Tablespoon garlic powder
2 teaspoons cumin
1 teaspoon black pepper
1 teaspoon chili powder (Add more if you want more heat!)
½ cup chopped green onions
Shredded cheese and sour cream to garnish (optional!)

In a large saucepan, heat your vegetable stock on medium, until it starts to bubble. Add your soya, and mix. Remove from the heat, and let the soya rehydrate in the stock. While that's happening, chop your onion and your peppers, fairly finely.

Over a medium heat, in a large pot, heat your oil, onions and peppers. Once the onions start to become translucent, add your garlic powder, pepper, cumin and chili powder. Add your tomatoes and your soya kernels - including any remaining stock in the saucepan. Reduce your heat to medium, and add your beans. Once your chili starts to bubble, reduce the heat to low, and simmer for an additional 10-15 minutes, uncovered.

Taste your chili to see if it needs more salt or chili powder.

Serve over rice, noodles or baked potatoes. Vegan cheddar cheese shreds are delicious for garnish if you're wanting to keep it entirely plant based.

Pulled Pork

As a native of Kansas City, barbeque is in my blood. Pulled Pork, however, was never part of my early culinary life - Kansas City barbeque was always more beef-centric, and pulled pork was much more of a Southeast American barbeque speciality. This can be either dressed with barbeque sauce, salsa verde, or any sauce you want! Choose your own adventure! You can do this in a pressure cooker, slow cooker, stovetop or in the oven.

What You Need:

- 3 lb. pork shoulder
- 1 medium yellow onion, chopped
- 1 medium bell pepper, chopped
- 2 Tablespoons minced fresh garlic, and 6 whole, peeled garlic cloves
- 2 Tablespoons vegetable oil
- 1 Tablespoon salt
- 1 teaspoon cumin
- 1 teaspoon chili powder
- 1 teaspoon paprika
- 1 teaspoon black pepper

Start by rinsing your pork shoulder, and stabbing your knife into the flesh 6 or 7 times - insert a garlic clove into each of the stabs. In a large cooking pot (or slow cooker), heat your vegetable oil, onion, bell pepper and garlic. While they're browning, sprinkle the pork with the salt, cumin, chili powder, paprika and black pepper. Pat the dry seasoning onto the pork.

When your onion, pepper and garlic are getting to a golden color, lay your pork roast, spice side up, onto the browning mixture. Slowly pour enough water into the pot to JUST cover the pork. Put on the lid, and turn the heat to high. When it starts to boil, stir the roast around in the vegetables, reduce the heat to low, and leave the lid propped open on the pot, so a small bit of the steam can get out. Set a timer for an hour. When the timer sounds, return to the pot, and with large tongs, turn the roast over in the pan, and set the timer for another hour. (If you're doing this in a pressure cooker, it usually takes 45 min to 1 hour, depending on how hot you're cooking it.)

After that next hour, test for doneness. You know it's ready then the meat falls apart without much effort. Pinch the roast with the tongs, and gently twist. If the meat comes apart easily, it's done. If it resists, it needs more time. Let it continue to simmer, and check it every 10 minutes or so until it's done. Let it rest in the broth for about 10 minutes. Using a slotted spoon, remove the meat from the pan, and transfer to a mixing bowl. Remove any bone pieces that may have come loose from the roast. Using two forks, back to back, shred the meat.

Add your favorite barbecue sauce to the shredded pork, or make tacos with it for carnitas.

Fried Chicken Tenders

One of the many, many horrifying things to emerge from 1990's restaurants is the obsession that every restaurant, no matter how fancy, MUST have a kids menu. Not every restaurant needs to cater to children, but even the poshest restaurants will come up with a bland macaroni and cheese, french fries, or chicken tenders, if it meant that their parents would come spend money in their establishment. These chicken tenders are an adult adaptation that children are all but guaranteed to hate.

But hey, this isn't for them.

What You Need:
2 lbs Chicken Tenders
1 cup buttermilk
1 Tablespoon garlic salt
½ cup hot sauce (Frank's Red Hot or similar)
1 ½ cups flour
1 Tablespoon garlic powder
1 Tablespoon onion powder
2 eggs
¼ cup milk
3 cups breadcrumbs or panko
1 Tablespoon dried thyme
1 teaspoon kosher salt
3 cups vegetable or peanut oil for frying

Start by rinsing your chicken tenders, and patting them dry with paper towels. In a large mixing bowl, whisk together your buttermilk, garlic salt and hot sauce. Drop in your chicken, and marinate for about 90 minutes, but no longer than 2 hours.

While your chicken is marinating, put your flour, garlic powder and onion powder in a large freezer bag. In a soup bowl, scramble your two eggs with the milk. In another bowl, mix your panko, thyme and salt. This is your workstation to bread your chicken. The flour in the freezer bag is step 1, the egg/milk mix is step two, and your panko is step 3 - Set a clean plate at the end to collect your breaded chicken pieces.

Remove your chicken from the marinade, and pour into a colander. Shake off the excess buttermilk, and drop your chicken - piece by piece - into the flour bag. Once all your chicken is in the flour, zip the bag closed, and shake it about, covering each piece. Remove each piece of chicken, shake off the excess flour, dip in the egg and milk, let the excess fall off, and roll it in the breadcrumbs. After it's well covered, let it rest on the plate.

You can, at this point, freeze the chicken and save it for later, or fry it immediately.

Ready to cook 'em? Heat your cooking oil to 350 degrees. Fry a few pieces of chicken at a time - don't overcrowd the pan! Cook each piece until the internal temperature reaches 165 degrees - about 7-8 minutes total. Turn the pieces after 3 minutes or so, for even cooking. Wait for your oil to return to full heat between batches - usually only about 30 seconds or so.

Serve with any number of the sauces barbeque, ranch, etc. or any from Chapter 5 - particularly the sambal or tzatziki.

Chicken & Rice Casserole

This is another marvelous, Midwestern comforting "Mom" dish that people either love, or hate. Or they pretend to hate, but secretly love. Casserole, in its many permutations, gained a rather unfair reputation as being artless and common. Which is, possibly, why I love it so much. It's an excellent opportunity to use up leftovers, and make them magnificent. A mediocre casserole is fine - it's food, and fills you up. But an elevated casserole is evocative of childhood happiness and can be truly something next level.

What You Need:
- 2 cups chopped, cooked chicken
- 2 cups cooked rice
- 2 ribs celery, chopped
- 1 medium onion, chopped
- 1 carrot, diced (or ½ cup frozen carrot dice)
- 2 cups roughly chopped mushrooms
- 4 tablespoons butter, cut into small chunks
- 1 teaspoon kosher salt
- 1 teaspoon minced garlic
- 1 Tablespoon dried Italian seasoning
- 2 Tablespoons flour
- 2 cups milk
- 1 cup shredded cheddar
- ¼ cup bread crumbs

Preheat oven to 350 degrees. Grease a 9" x 12" roasting pan. In a large mixing bowl, add your cooked rice, chicken and ½ cup of cheddar cheese.

In a large saute pan, add half of your butter (2 Tablespoons), onions, carrots and celery. Saute until your onions are translucent, and starting to brown. Add your mushrooms, garlic and Italian seasoning. Mix together, and sprinkle your flour across the mixture, and stir throughout the veggie mix. Let the mixture cook for a minute or two, then add your milk. Using a whisk or slotted spoon, blend the milk into the mixture until it smoothes. Remove from the heat, and pour over the cheese, rice and chicken. Stir it all together, and pour into the roasting pan.

Smooth the top, and sprinkle the remaining cheese, and breadcrumbs. Dot small pieces of your remaining butter across the top. Bake for 30 minutes. Check on it - is it browned on top to your satisfaction? If the center heated through? If not, leave it for another 10 minutes. Once it's done to your satisfaction, remove from the oven, and allow it to rest for at least 10 minutes before serving.

Sesame Glazed Salmon

I've always considered this one of those delicious, special event foods. But, it's only a "special event" because salmon is criminally expensive when you're a broke artist. For several years, I lived in Seattle where the salmon is legendary. Indeed, in late May and June, the salmon from the Copper River area in Alaska becomes available and is truly the best salmon possible. But that nosebleed price tag is quite a bitter pill to swallow when you're barely making ends meet. However, I'd still rather save my pennies and have truly amazing salmon once or twice a year than ever resort to the canned variety.

What You Need:
4 filets of Salmon
1 onion, sliced thin
¼ cup brown sugar
¼ cup soy sauce
2 tablespoons sesame oil
1 tablespoon minced garlic
½ teaspoon ground ginger
3 green onions, minced
Pinch of black pepper

Preheat your oven to 350 degrees.

Let's start on your glaze. In a small mixing bowl, whisk together your brown sugar, soy sauce, sesame oil, garlic and ginger. Let it rest a moment, and whisk again until your sugar is mostly dissolved.

Oil a baking dish, and layer your onions across the bottom. Evenly space your salmon filets on the onions. Spoon half of your marinade over your filets, and sprinkle with black pepper. Bake your salmon, uncovered, for 10 minutes. Remove the salmon from the oven, and spoon the remaining marinade over the top of the salmon, and return to the oven for an additional 5-10 minutes. Remove from the oven, and let the salmon rest for 5 minutes before serving. Garnish with minced green onion.

SIDEBAR: *A simple, tasty, and probably slightly healthier alternative, if you're looking to avoid the glaze, is to simply bake the salmon on the bed of onions, drizzle some olive oil across the top of the salmon, sprinkle with salt and cover your filets with a dozen or so fronds of fresh dill. Pour ¼ cup of water in the pan, and cover the dish with foil. Bake for 15-20 minutes. Let it rest and serve with the salt roasted potatoes from Chapter 8.*

Roasted Chicken Provençal

This is a deceptively simple, but always impressive dish. If there's ONE recipe that sealed my love for French country cookery, it would likely be this - or Coq au Vin. For that, look to Julia Child - I can add nothing to the masters there.

What You Need:
1 chicken, whole or in parts (completely thawed)
¼ cup minced garlic
4 Tablespoons butter, softened (not melted!)
1 Tablespoon dried oregano
1 Tablespoon dried thyme
1 Tablespoon dried marjoram or savory
2 tablespoons rosemary, minced fine
1 teaspoon salt
½ teaspoon black pepper
1 lemon, cut into slices
16 new potatoes, cut in half

Preheat your oven to 475 degrees.

Rinse your chicken, inside and outside, and pat dry with a paper towel. Let it rest on the counter until it's reached room temperature. In a small mixing bowl, mash together your butter, garlic, herbs, salt and pepper to create a paste. Rub the outside of your chicken parts with your butter mixture. If you're doing a whole chicken, rub some on the inside of the cavity as well. Sprinkle everything with a little more salt, and lay your lemon slices across the chicken. If you're doing a whole chicken, cut your lemon half into wedges and half in slices. Insert the wedges into the cavity, and the slices on top of the chicken.

Don't be afraid of the butter. The butter is your friend.

> **PRO TIP:** *If you're making a whole chicken, make sure to check the inside of the cavity to see if the butcher has left some internal organs. Remove those before you roast the chicken.*

Lay your chicken, meat side up, in the roasting pan. Insert potato halves around the chicken to fill in the spaces. Roast the chicken and potatoes at 475 for 15 minutes. Reduce the heat to 375, and roast for an additional 20 minutes. Check the temperature on your chicken - if the internal temperature has reached 180 degrees, they're ready. Let everything rest for about 5 minutes, and serve.

Penne Arrabiata

This is traditionally a spicy, meatless pasta that is so satisfying when you want a light, but substantial meal. The garlic is really the star of this show, so don't skimp on it. If you're not sure about garlic, or are serving people who are less enthusiastic about garlic, I'd suggest you make something different. It can be VERY confronting, in terms of flavor, but it's one of my favorite ways to showcase the magic that is garlic and tomato. It also makes a lovely side dish for steak or pork roast, if you really want to serve meat with it.

WHAT YOU NEED:

30 cloves of garlic, peeled (Yes, 30!)
1 cup olive oil
2 large cans of diced tomatoes (28 oz cans)
1 Tablespoon fennel seeds (optional, but it's a nice addition!)
1 Tablespoon dried chili flakes (add more if you like more heat!)
½ cup chopped pepperoncini
1 teaspoon salt
½ cup chopped fresh basil
1 lb. Penne pasta
Parmesan to garnish

In a large pot, heat your olive oil on medium. Once your oil is heated, add in your garlic cloves. Let them simmer for a moment - once you start to see small bubbles, reduce the heat to low. Let them continue to cook for about 5-10 minutes, or until they're soft enough to easily smash with the back of a spoon. This is adding flavor to the oil, and slowly cooking the garlic cloves to a bright, sweeter flavor. Once they're soft, scoop them out of the oil, and set them aside in a small mixing bowl to cool - cover the bowl tightly with foil. Add your tomatoes, pepperoncini, fennel seed, chili flakes and salt to the oil, and heat over low for about 15 minutes.

Take you garlic cloves, and either puree them in a food processor, or smash them thoroughly with a spoon, or masher, until you have a fairly smooth paste. Scoop them back into the tomato mixture, and stir well.

In a separate large pot, heat 2 quarts of water to a boil, and cook your penne just until it's not QUITE entirely cooked. With a slotted spoon, scoop the almost cooked pasta into the sauce. If the sauce seems super thick, add a ladle full of the pasta water, and incorporate it into the mixture. Add water until the sauce and pasta mix seems ALMOST too watery. Let the pasta simmer in the sauce for about 10 minutes, or until the pasta is cooked, and the sauce consistency is where you like it.

Remove from the heat, and stir in your basil. Garnish each dish with parmesan cheese and cracked black pepper.

Crustless Veggie Quiche

This is one of those amazingly easy recipes that seems SUPER impressive when you serve this at brunch, but never really breakfast. I say that, only because I've never actually made one of these before 9:00 a.m., but I suppose you could if you're that sort of morning person who cooked breakfast. Serve this with mixed greens and a citrus vinaigrette - it's the perfect balance to the richness of the quiche. And leftovers keep well in the fridge for a couple days.

What You Need:

Filling
6 Eggs, scrambled
¼ cup milk
1 teaspoon garlic salt
1 shallot
1 Tablespoon of olive oil
1 small can diced tomato & chilis, drained
4 cups fresh spinach leaves, chopped
1 small russet potato, diced
1 cup water
½ cup parmesan cheese
1 cup panko or seasoned breadcrumbs

Take your diced potato, and put it in a small saucepan with a cup of water. Heat it on high, until it starts to simmer. Once the simmering begins, reduce the heat to low and let it simmer for 5 minutes. Remove from the heat, and strain off the water. The potatoes should be slightly softened. Set aside to cool. Preheat your oven to 375 degrees.

Mince your shallots, drain your diced tomatoes and chilis. In a large saute pan, heat your shallots with a Tablespoon of olive oil. Once they begin to sizzle, add your tomatoes and chilis. Stir and heat for a minute, then add your potatoes and chopped spinach. Saute until the spinach wilts, then remove from the heat.

Grab a pie dish, or tin, and lightly oil the inside. Coat the inside of the dish with your breadcrumbs, sticking them to the oiled surface. In a mixing bowl, whisk your eggs, milk and garlic salt.

In the bottom of the disk, spoon in half of your spinach mixture, and sprinkle half your cheese over that. Pour your eggs into the dish, over the vegetables and cheese. Spoon the remaining vegetable mixture into the eggs. Sprinkle on the remaining cheese. Use a fork to distribute the vegetables evenly in the dish.

Your dish might be VERY full, so be careful when moving it to the oven. Bake in the center of the oven, uncovered for 20 minutes. Turn your pan, and bake for 10 minutes more. If the top is starting to brown, then you're done. If not, bake in 5 minute increments until the top has set and is browned to your satisfaction.

Risotto With Squash And Peas

Another dish from country Italian cuisine - this is a magnificent and impressive dish. It also has quite a few steps to it, so definitely not one you want to start unless you're prepared to settle in for an hour and a half in the kitchen. But it is SO very worth it. Ignore your phone. Put the kids in front of the TV. You don't want any distractions here.

What You Need:
1 ½ Cups Arborio Rice
2 Tablespoons olive oil
2 Tablespoons butter
1 medium onion, minced fine
1 quart chicken or vegetable stock
1 Tablespoon dried oregano
1 Tablespoon fresh minced garlic
1 butternut squash
1 cup frozen peas
1 cup parmesan cheese
¼ cup half and half
½ cup chopped fresh parsley
1 lemon, juice and zest

Preheat your oven to 400 degrees.

Cut your butternut squash in half, vertically. With a spoon, scoop out the seeds and loose pulp. Brush the cut side of the squash with a little olive oil, and sprinkle with salt and pepper. On a foil-lined baking sheet, place the squash halves, cut side down. Bake for approximately 45 minutes. Once you can easily slip a knife into the flesh of the squash, it's done - set it aside to cool.

While your squash is baking, let's start on the risotto. In a saucepan, pour in your stock, oregano and garlic. Heat it over a medium flame - if it starts to bubble, reduce the heat to low. It doesn't need to be HOT - just warm - about 140 degrees. .

In a large pot, heat 2 Tablespoons of olive oil, and 2 Tablespoons of butter on medium heat. Toss in your onion, with a sprinkling of salt, and stir it around until it starts to become a pale golden color. Pour in your rice, and stir it into the mixture. Reduce your heat to low. The rice kernels start to become slightly translucent, and make a gentle "tinkling" sound around the bottom of the pot as they absorb the butter and oil. As things start to look slightly dry in the pot, add a ladle of your warm stock. Stir it into the rice and onion mixture, using a silicone spatula. Scrape the bottom and sides of the pot to make sure that every-thing is mixing well. Let the broth cook down, add another ladle of stock, and stir in again. Repeat this ladling and cooking cycle, over and over again - this can take as little as 30 minutes and up to an hour. This will slowly cook the rice, as it absorbs the stock. Do not rush this process.

Once your rice looks creamy, and is tender (spoon out a bit and taste it), then the rice is done. Add your parmesan, and half and half, and stir into the rice. Once that's well incorporated, stir in your parsley, peas, lemon juice and lemon zest. Taste it again, to determine if you need more salt. The parmesan brings a LOT of salt to the party, so you may not need to add any.

Back to your squash! Scoop out the cooked squash from the skin, and cut it into 1" chunks - they'll be a little soft, so if they don't have perfect edges, it's totally okay. Drop your squash chunks into the risotto and fold in. Put the lid on, and turn off the heat. Let the residual heat of the risotto warm the squash through.

Serve with an additional sprinkling of fresh parsley. This is excellent as a main, or as a side dish with roast pork loin, or steak. Sit back and graciously accept the accolades that will be lauded upon you for making risotto from scratch..

SIDEBAR: *Look, if your first risotto isn't perfect, that's totally normal. It takes some practice, and overcooking is probably the most common mistake. The risotto should be creamy, and somewhat thick, but not so thick that you can stand a spoon up in it. Undercooked risotto will be runny, and possibly a little crunchy from undercooked rice. Overcooked risotto will be thick and mushy, and you may not be able to distinguish individual rice grains. If it doesn't work, try it again. And again. Once you have this recipe mastered, you'll be unstoppable.*

Mushroom and Leek Strudel

We have those wacky Habsburgs to thank for the popularization of strudel. Usually it's a dessert - most often the apple variety - but this savory version is an excellent lunch or dinner. If you aren't able to find leeks, worry not - just substitute a half and half combination of shallots and green onions. You can use any sort of mushrooms that you like in this recipe.

What You Need:

Pastry
2 cups flour
2 Tablespoons butter, very cold
2 eggs
1 teaspoon baking powder
1 teaspoon sugar
½ teaspoon salt
¼ cup water, very cold

Filling
4 cups mushrooms, roughly chopped
1 cup leeks, thinly sliced (just the white part, and the softer parts of the green.)
4 tablespoons butter
½ cup dry white wine or dry vermouth
1 tablespoon dried oregano or marjoram
1 tablespoon minced garlic
2 teaspoons Worcestershire sauce
½ teaspoon salt
½ cup chopped parsley
½ cup feta crumbles, or shredded mozzarella
2 Tablespoons melted butter

Start with your pastry. In a stand mixer, mix together your eggs, sugar and butter - mix until you have a creamy, well incorporated mixture. Add your flour and baking powder in small doses. Add the water, bit by bit until the dough comes together into a smooth ball. Remove from the mixer and roll it around a floured surface, wrap it in plastic wrap, and refrigerate it for 30 minutes.

While the pastry is chilling, let's start on the filling. In a large saute pan, melt your butter over medium heat. Add your leeks, garlic and oregano. As your leeks start to soften, sprinkle on your salt. Add your mushrooms and mix thoroughly. Pour over your wine and sprinkle over the Worcestershire sauce. Stir until the wine cooks down, and the mushrooms have softened. Remove from the heat, and transfer to a mixing bowl to cool.

Preheat your oven to 375 degrees. Oil a baking sheet liberally.

Back to the pastry! Remove from the refrigerator, and add a little more flour to your floured surface. You'll want to roll out your dough to about ¼" thick. Fold the dough over itself in half, then half again, and roll it out again. Do this two more times, and roll it out to be a rectangle about 12" x 18". Lay your pastry on the baking sheet.

Spoon the mushroom mixture in the center of the pastry, in a smaller rectangle about 12" long, and 6" wide. Sprinkle the feta and parsley over the mushroom mixture. Fold the pastry in on the short sides. Then, fold over the bottom of the pastry, and roll it forward. Stretch the end of the pastry over the end to seal. Center the pastry on the baking sheet. Brush the outside of the pastry with butter. Poke the top of the pastry with the tip of a knife to make a few ½ slits in the top of the dough.

Bake the pastry for approximately 35-40 minutes, or until the pastry is well browned. Allow it to cool about 15 minutes before serving. Cut into slices to serve.

Easy Cottage Pie

This is a perfect winter dish when you want something easy, that can be leftovers for a few days. But lamb isn't always that affordable, so beef is a great substitution. If ground beef or ground lamb is more available, you can definitely use that instead. This is one of few recipes in this book that uses pre-packaged ingredients - but sometimes you want to put together something tasty that's also quick.

What You Need:

2-3 lb.. boneless chuck roast or 4-5 lb. boneless leg of lamb roast
1 cup red wine
6 med. potatoes *peeled, cut into 1" cubes*
1 cup chopped onions
2 ribs celery, chopped small
2 cups of frozen peas & carrots mix
1 package brown gravy mix
dissolved in 1 cup cold water

1 teaspoon kosher salt
½ teaspoon black pepper
½ teaspoon rosemary, *finely chopped*
4 Tablespoons butter
1 Tablespoon fine minced garlic
¼ cup fine minced green onion

If you're using a beef chuck roast or leg of lamb: On high heat, melt 2 Tablespoons of butter, add ½ cup onion, half of your celery and your roast. Add just enough water to cover. When your water starts to boil, reduce your heat to low/medium. Lamb should take 1 - 1½ hours. Beef chuck roast should take slightly longer. Once the meat easily tears apart, it's done. Remove from the pot, and chop it down into chunks, and remove any bone pieces that might be present. Set aside to cool.

In a large saucepan, simmer your potatoes in just enough water to cover. Simmer on medium heat until the potatoes are softened. While your potatoes are cooking, let's start on the filling.

In a large saute pan, saute the other ½ cup onion in a little olive oil. Add the remaining celery, garlic. If you're using ground beef or lamb, add it to the pan and brown it. Add your rosemary and black pepper. If needs be, drain off any excess fat or moisture from the meat mixture. Reduce heat to low, then add your peas and carrots. Add your gravy mixture, stir well, and leave it to simmer. Mix slowly to let the gravy thicken. Once the gravy has thickened, remove from the heat.

In a stand mixer, beat your potatoes with 4 Tablespoons of butter, salt and the green onions, until mostly smooth. In a well-buttered casserole, or souffle dish, use ¾ of your mashed potatoes to line the dish like a pie crust - about ½-¾ inch thick all around. Pour in your filling, and top with the remaining potatoes - smooth out the top of your potatoes. Drag the back of your fork across the top of the potatoes to create lines. The potatoes DO NOT have to be perfect - rustic style is perfect here. The fork patterns on top will crisp nicely so the surface will have something of a "twice baked potato" texture.

Dot the top of the potatoes with ½ teaspoon chunks of butter. Move the dish onto a baking sheet. Bake for 40 minutes or until the top of the potatoes are browned. Allow the pie to cool for 15 minutes or so before serving.

- CHAPTER 11 -

Desserts

Cake is probably my favorite food group of all. Is there any better way to round out a meal than with a delicious sweet something? If you're looking for something inexpensive to make for an office potluck, see if making dessert is an option. Now, to be certain, desserts can also become extravagantly expensive if you really want them to be. But, something as simple as delicious sugar cookies can be easy and inexpensive to make.

Also, note that I haven't included recipes for some things - for instance, I haven't included a recipe for chocolate chip cookies here. Frankly, it's only because I can't really improve upon the Nestle Toll House recipe. It's pretty perfect as it is. Banana pudding? The one that everyone's mom made with the vanilla wafer cookies is pretty much ideal. But I've included recipes that are, hopefully, unique enough to impress friends, but not so intimidating that you won't want to experiment with them.

Some of the ingredients aren't necessarily things you'll have around the house all the time - molasses, allspice, cloves, etc. - so if you need to buy them specifically for these recipes, look for less expensive options. Fortunately, around the holidays, you can find great deals, even at your local grocery store for many of these ingredients. Molasses does keep for about a year if kept in a cool, dry cabinet. And many spices can be acquired in smaller quantities so you don't have to shell out a ton of money just for one recipe.

The Easiest Shortbread Cookies

When you want a simple sweet, this doesn't get much simpler. Always a nice treat to have around tea time, or when people come over. It's only 3 basic ingredients, unless you want to cover them in chocolate... which is always a welcome upgrade.

What You Need:
   1 cup butter, softened
   ½ cup sugar
   2 cups flour

Preheat your oven to 325 degrees. Line a baking sheet with parchment or foil.

Cream together your butter and sugar until well incorporated. Mix in your flour until you've created a dense dough. Shape into a circle, and press into a ½" thick round. Cut it into 8 wedges, like pizza. With a fork, stab each wedge twice, to let steam escape. Push the wedges together into the circle. Sprinkle with a little more sugar, and bake for 35-40 minutes.

Once they're golden brown, remove from the oven and allow them to cool completely on a wire rack. As they're cooling, slice through the scored parts to separate the wedges.

Spicy Ginger Cookies

A holiday favorite to be certain, but also a marvelous sweet treat to keep around the house any time of year. These are my favorite cookies to serve with tea.

What You Need:

1 stick of butter (I'd stick with regular butter here, if possible!)
½ cup brown sugar (either dark or light, but dark does add some extra deliciousness!)
¼ cup molasses
1 egg
2 cups flour
1 teaspoon baking soda
1 teaspoon kosher salt
2 teaspoons ground ginger
1 teaspoon fresh grated ginger (optional, but delicious!)
1 teaspoon cinnamon
½ teaspoon ground cloves
½ teaspoon nutmeg
¼ teaspoon ground allspice

In your mixing bowl, soften your butter. Add your brown sugar, and beat the butter and sugar together until it's well incorporated and starting to become fluffy. (This will involve scraping down the sides of your bowl a few times.)

Add the molasses, then sprinkle the salt, baking soda and spices across the mixture. Mix those in, and add the egg. Mix everything until well incorporated. While your mixer is on low, add your flour a few tablespoons at a time until it's all well mixed. Once the dough comes together, scrape down everything from the sides of the bowl, and mix again until everything comes together.

Scoop the dough into an airtight container, or a bowl with plastic wrap, and leave it in the refrigerator for at least 3 hours. Dough keeps well in the refrigerator for up to a week.

After your dough has chilled, and you're ready to bake, preheat your oven to 350 degrees.

In a small bowl, pour in ¼ cup sugar. On a baking sheet, line with baking parchment or use non-stick spray. Using a spoon or small scoop, measure out balls of dough (approximately 1 inch in diameter). Roll into smooth balls, and roll them in the bowl of sugar. Once you've lined up your dough balls on the baking sheet - at least an inch or so apart, flatten them slightly using your fingers or the bottom of a drinking glass. Your flattened dough circles should be about a ½ inch thick.

Bake the cookies for about 10 minutes. Remove the pan from the oven, and rest it on a cooling rack or on the stovetop. After they've cooled for about 3 minutes, remove the cookies from the pan, move them onto a plate to finish cooling.

Easy Lemon Curd

Okay, his recipe took some practice, but even the "imperfect" versions that came out while I was working on perfecting it were still pretty darned good. This takes very few ingredients, and some patience. This curd is perfect as the filling in a fruit tart, or just served on a scone with butter. A food processor is best here, but it isn't impossible to do by hand.

What You Need:
2 cups sugar
4 large lemons (or 5-6 smaller) - remove the zest, and juice the lemons
1 stick butter
5 large eggs
Dash of salt

In your food processor, combine your sugar and lemon zest and pulse until the zest is pulverized into the sugar. In your mixer, or with a hand mixer, cream your butter and the lemon/sugar mixture. Add your eggs slowly, then incorporate your lemon juice into the mix.

Pour the mixture into a saucepan, and turn your stove heat to medium/low. With a wooden or silicone spoon, stir gently but constantly. If it starts bubbling quickly, reduce the heat to low. Keep stirring - you don't want it to stick to the bottom of the pan.

The curd will start to thicken, and become smooth. Once it's smoothed out and thickened, remove from the heat, and pour into heat-proof jars, or a bowl, and allow to cool for a couple minutes, then move to the refrigerator. Allow to chill for at least 2 hours before serving.

The Cheesecake

I call this recipe "The Cheesecake" because there is literally no other cheesecake recipe that I ever look to. Now, this is not a "light" cheesecake. This is a rich, marvelous and decadent cheesecake that isn't TOO sweet, so it's a perfect conveyance for chocolate, any number of fruit sauces or the lemon curd that appears on page 157. Crust options are infinite, depending on the taste that you're looking to create. Many thanks to my friend Sara for giving me the formulation that gave birth to this recipe.

What You Need:

30 gingersnaps or vanilla wafer cookies
½ stick butter, melted
24 oz. cream cheese (three regular size boxes!)
3 eggs
1 can sweetened condensed milk
½ cup sugar
¼ cup flour, sifted
1 teaspoon vanilla (or almond extract)
1 Tablespoon lemon zest
1 Tablespoon lemon juice
1 cup hot water

In a mixing bowl, let the cream cheese soften for an hour or so until it's near room temperature.

While your cream cheese is softening, start on your crust. Take your gingersnaps (or other cookies) and crush them in a bag, or pulverize them in a food processor, until they're crumbs. Combine the crumbs with the melted butter, and set aside for a couple minutes to let the butter soak into the cookie crumbs.

In a 9-10" springform pan, spray the pan with non-stick spray, then spread out the butter and crumbs, and press into the pan to create a smooth crust, bringing the crust up the sides of the pan - it's okay if it doesn't go all the way to the top of the pan. Wrap the bottom of your springform pan with foil, and place it on a jelly roll pan, or baking sheet that has a lip around it. Preheat your oven to 350 degrees.

In your mixing bowl, add your eggs and condensed milk to your cream cheese, and mix on low until everything is well incorporated, and smooth. Add your sugar and flour. Mix on low/medium. As your mixer is incorporating everything together, add your vanilla, lemon zest and lemon juice. Once everything is well mixed and smooth, turn off your mixer and scrape down the sides of your bowl, and mix again for a moment to incorporate everything together.

Tap your mixing bowl on the countertop - this will help release bubbles that may be trapped in the cheesecake batter. Slowly pour the cheesecake batter onto the crust. Gently drag a butter knife through your cheesecake batter (don't hit the crust!) to help release more air bubbles.

Place the cake pan, on the baking sheet, into the oven. While it's IN the oven, pour the hot water into the baking sheet, so that it surrounds the foil base of the springform pan. It should only come up about ½ - ¾ inch of the cheesecake pan.

Bake at 350 for about 40 minutes - baking time depends on humidity, your oven, the orbit of the moon, the mood of the stove... After that time has lapsed, gently slide out the pan and give it a little shake. Does the top of the cheesecake shimmy? Then it probably needs an extra few minutes. The top of the cheesecake will go from shiny, to a matte finish. Once the edges are golden brown, and the cake starts to pull away from the sides of the pan, take it out of the oven and rest it on a cooling rack. As it cools, it will pull away more from the sides of the pan. If you see parts of the crust clinging to the side, as it cools, use the back of a butter knife to gently release it from the pan.

After it's cooled to room temperature, slowly release the springform and let the cake rest until entirely cooled. Once it's cooled to the touch, refrigerate or freeze the cheesecake until it's ready to serve. It keeps nicely in the refrigerator for up to 4 days, or freezes well for up to 6 months.

Apricot & Blueberry Clafoutis

This is one of those fancy pants French dishes that's incredibly delicious and surprisingly easy to make. It's something between a set custard pie and a soft cake, and is delicious served with ice cream. Traditionally it's made with fresh cherries, but you can really use any sort of stone fruit or berries. It only keeps for a day or so in the refrigerator, so it's ideal for a dinner party where you won't want much in the way of leftovers.

What You Need:

3 eggs
1 ¼ cups of whole milk
½ cup flour, sifted
½ cup sugar, set aside 3 Tablespoons
¼ cup amaretto (optional, but delicious)
1 teaspoon vanilla
4 apricots (peeled, pitted and cut into 6 wedges)
2 cups fresh blueberries (rinsed, and spread on a clean towel to dry)

Butter a 10x13 glass baking dish (metal isn't recommended here). Preheat your oven to 350 degrees.

In a blender, mix your eggs, milk, flour, sugar, amaretto and vanilla. Blend until smooth, and slightly foamy. If you don't have a blender, then you can certainly mix it by hand with a whisk.

Pour half of the mixture into the bottom of the baking dish until you have about a ¼ inch layer on the bottom of the dish. Set aside the remaining batter.

Bake this thin layer for about 5-6 minutes just until it starts to set. Remove the baking dish from the oven. Over the batter, make one layer of the apricots - evenly distributed across the batter. Sprinkle the blueberries across the apricots, and sprinkle with the 3 Tablespoons of sugar.

Pour the remaining batter over the fruit, and return to the oven for about 45 minutes. Once the edges are just starting to brown and the clafoutis has puffed up a bit, and a knife poked into the center comes out clean.

Let it cool to room temperature, slice into squares and sprinkle with powdered sugar to serve.

Chewy Peanut Butter Cookies

These are one of those amazing, anytime treats that everyone seems to love. Coating these in chocolate, adding chocolate chips or placing a chocolate kiss on each is also a nice way to bring these familiar treats to a new level. I also tend to underbake these by a couple minutes, to keep them as soft and chewy as possible.

What You Need:
1 ½ cups flour
½ teaspoon baking soda
Pinch of salt
1 stick of butter or margarine
¾ c brown sugar
¼ c white sugar
1 cup peanut butter (I like smooth here, but you do you!)
1 egg
1 teaspoon vanilla

In a mixing bowl, cream together your butter, vanilla and sugars until they're well mixed and fluffy. Mix in your egg, then your peanut butter. Mix until smooth.

Sprinkle the baking soda across the mixture, and spoon in your flour a few tablespoons at a time until all is well incorporated. Once it's all well mixed, cover the dough and refrigerate for about 30 minutes.

While your dough is in the refrigerator, Heat your oven to 350 degrees, and line two baking sheets with parchment, or non-stick spray.

Scoop and shape your dough into balls about the size of ping pong balls (1 ½ inch in diameter) and spread them out on your baking sheet - leave about 3 inches between each. Flatten each dough ball with a fork, to leave the familiar markings on top.

Bake for approximately 10-12 minutes (depending on your oven). Once the sides of the cookies appear dry, and the dough has spread slightly, remove from the oven, and let them rest ON the baking sheets. The residual heat will help them finish cooking.

If they're too doughy, and underdone, return them to the oven for a minute at a time until they're baked they way you like them.

Churritos

When I think of a churro, I immediately envision those tree branch sized sticks that you get from amusement parks and carnivals. But these I like to make smaller versions, to be roughly the size of a puffed cheese snack. It's helpful to have a piping bag with a large star-shaped tip. This creates those ridges that hold sugar and cinnamon more easily, but smooth sided churros are still delicious. They're a perfect party snack when you want a little something sweet on the table.

What You Need:
1 cup water
1 cup flour, sifted
1 egg
½ stick butter, cut into small pieces
½ cup, plus 1 Tablespoon sugar
1 teaspoon vanilla
1 ½ teaspoons cinnamon
¼ teaspoon salt
1 quart vegetable oil

Heat your vegetable oil in a saucepan over medium heat.

Lightly beat your egg with the vanilla and set aside. Mix the ½ cup of sugar and cinnamon in a separate bowl, and set aside.

In a separate saucepan, mix your water, butter, 1 Tablespoon of sugar and salt. Heat just until boiling, then remove from the heat and stir in the flour to create a ball of dough. Transfer dough to a mixing bowl, and with a stand mixer or by hand, stir the dough to release some of the heat, then beat the egg and vanilla into the dough - don't stop stirring, you want to incorporate the egg (If you beat too slowly the egg with scramble and become chunky). Once the egg is well incorporated, the egg will be a smooth dough. Let it rest for about 10 minutes while you prepare your piping bag with a large star tip.

Scoop the dough into the piping bag - it will still be warm - and pipe small pieces of dough into the hot oil. If it doesn't start frying immediately when it hits the oil, wait for a few minutes until the oil comes up to heat (about 325-250 degrees.) If it fries and browns within a couple seconds, scoop it out to drain on a paper towel-lined mixing bowl. If it's frying too quickly, reduce the heat slightly.

Fry the churros until all the dough is used. Don't overcrowd the fryer, cooking a few at a time. Once they're all fried, sprinkle the cooked churros with the sugar and cinnamon mixture and gently toss them around until everything is coated.

Serve immediately.

Spicy Banana Bread

When it comes to banana breads, I'm often ambivalent. I've had some that are TRULY marvelous - flavorful and moist, in both loaf and muffin forms. I've also had some that are grey, flavorless lumps - so dry and dense as to be used as a doorstop. The easiest mistake to make is to overestimate how much banana you have to add to the recipe. As bananas age, they do shrink, so if you have four VERY brown bananas, that will be far less than four slightly browning bananas... make sense? So for this recipe, I've tried to keep the measurements entirely by volume, and not quantity. As you play with this recipe, adjust the ratio of ingredients - but moisture is the most important. Think one egg to every cup of mashed bananas, and adjust accordingly. This recipe also adapts nicely to muffins - just reduce your bake time slightly.

What You Need:
2 cups mashed bananas
2 cups flour
2 large eggs
1 stick butter or margarine
½ cup brown sugar
½ cup white sugar
¼ cup molasses
1 ½ teaspoons baking soda
1 ½ teaspoons baking powder
2 Tablespoons fresh grated ginger (optional)
1 teaspoon cinnamon
½ teaspoon nutmeg
½ teaspoon cloves (ground)
½ teaspoon allspice
½ teaspoon ground ginger

Preheat your oven to 350 degrees. Butter two loaf pans.

Mix together your flour, baking powder and soda, and set them aside in a separate bowl.

In another mixing bowl, cream together your butter, banana, molasses, eggs, sugars, ginger and the other spices. Slowly fold in your flour mixture, about ½ cup at a time, until all is well incorporated, and you have a mostly smooth batter - if you have a few little lumps of banana, that's totally okay, just make sure you don't have any lumps of flour. Just smash those out with the back of a mixing spoon.

Evenly divide the batter between the two loaf pans, and bake for about 40 minutes. Poke a toothpick into the thickest part of the center of the loaf - once it comes out dry, your loaf is done. Remove from the oven, and let it cool in the pan entirely. Once it's cooled, remove the loaf from the pan, and serve.

Flourless Chocolate Torte

This is a deeply impressive recipe that involves only five ingredients. It also calls for whisky, but if you only have brandy or something like amaretto, any of those will work well, too. Now, if you have a hand or stand mixer, this recipe will be much easier - especially the parts where you have to whip the egg whites. If you've ever done that by hand, you'll know that a little mechanical help will make you much happier at the end of the day.

What You Need:

4 eggs, separated
⅓ cup sugar (superfine is great here if you have it!)
1 cup semi-sweet chocolate chips
1 stick butter, cut into small pieces
1 Tablespoon whisky

Preheat your oven to 350 degrees. Line a springform pan with parchment, and butter the pan and the parchment.

On the stovetop, heat 3 inches of water in a saucepan until simmering lightly. Reduce the heat to the lowest setting. Set a metal mixing bowl on top of the pan, and put the butter in the bowl. Let the butter melt. Once the butter is liquid, add your chocolate, and start stirring your chocolate to start melting it into the butter. Continue stirring until the chocolate and butter are well mixed.

In another mixing bowl, mix half of the sugar and the four egg yolks, and whisk aggressively until the mixture becomes a paler yellow color. Remove the chocolate bowl from the saucepan. In a THIN stream, pour your egg and sugar mixture into the chocolate, while constantly stirring the chocolate. (This might be a good time to have a friend help you.) Add your whiskey and stir into the chocolate mixture.

In a stand mixer, or with a hand mixer... (or by hand with a whisk if you're feeling strong!) Whisk your egg whites until they form firm peaks. Sprinkle in the remaining sugar as the mixer continues to beat the egg whites. Once the sugar is added, the peaks will become glossy and firm.

Scoop about a third of your egg whites into the chocolate mix, and fold gently together. Once they're well incorporated, scoop in the remaining egg whites and fold everything together until it's all well combined. Pour into the baking pan and with a spoon, smooth out the surface. Bake for approximately 20 minutes until the torte starts to crackle a bit on top. It'll be done, when a toothpick comes out clean when inserted into the middle.

Allow it to cool completely on the counter. Remove it from the springform pan, and transfer to a plate, and wrap loosely with plastic wrap. Refrigerate the cake for at least an hour or two before serving. Serve with fresh berries and whipped cream.

Shredded Apple Pie

This is one of those ancient recipes that I truly can't improve upon. This recipe came from my great-grandmother, so it's at LEAST 100 years old. In the last ten decades, no one along the way could manage to make it better. The only change I've made is to use a food processor to make the crust.

What You Need:

The Crust:
2 cups flour
1 cup shortening
1 teaspoon salt
½ cup ice cold water

The Filling:
4 green Granny Smith apples, cores removed
1 stick butter, melted
½ cup sugar
1 teaspoon vanilla
1 ½ teaspoon cinnamon
½ teaspoon nutmeg
¼ cup flour
1 egg, scrambled

Let's start with the crust. Put the flour in the food processor with the teaspoon of salt. Turn on the food processor to the lowest setting. Pinch pieces of the shortening into the flour as it's blending. Once the dough resembles damp crumbles, turn off the food processor.

Dump the flour into a large mixing bowl. Using one hand, start kneading the flour mixture. A tablespoon or so at a time, add the water into the mix. Knead the water into the mixture. Keep adding water until you have a fairly dense dough, that isn't too sticky, but not too dry.

Flatten the crust into a square-ish shape, then can fold it over, top to bottom. Use a little bit of flour on the outside of the dough if it gets sticky. Turn the dough ¼ to the right. Roll out the dough slightly, and fold again. Turn the dough again, and fold again. Do this three more times. Once the dough has been folded for the seventh time, wrap it in plastic wrap, and move it to the refrigerator to chill while you work on the filling.

Take your apples, and remove the cores and stems. You can also just cut them in half and cut out the centers, the stem, seeds and blossom end. Don't worry about peeling the apple, just grate them on the large side of your cheese grater. Move them to a strainer to let the excess moisture drain out.

In a large mixing bowl, add your shredded apples, pour your melted butter over the apples. Sprinkle the sugar, spices and flour over the apples. Stir everything together and allow it to rest while you roll out your crust. Preheat your oven to 400 degrees.

Butter a pie pan, or Pyrex pie plate. Take your pie crust and cut into half. Roll out half until it's about ¼ inch thick. Press it into the bottom of the pie dish, leaving the rest hanging over the edge. Pour in your apple mixture, and press firmly into the crust - squeezing out any air bubbles.

Roll out your second piece of dough, and lay over the top of the pie. Using a knife, cut off the excess crust. Using a fork, go around the crust and seal the top and bottom crusts together. Cut 8 slits into the crust, so that one cut will be on each slice of the pie. Brush the egg across the top crust, and sprinkle with a little bit of sugar.

Set the pie onto a baking sheet (to catch any overflow). Bake the pie for about 15 minutes, turn the pie halfway around in the oven, reduce your heat to 350 degrees, and continue to bake for another 30 minutes. Once the crust is a rich golden brown, and the filling is bubbling, remove it from the oven, and let it rest until it's cooled.

Serve with whipped or ice cream.

- CHAPTER 12 -

Additional Notes

Kitchen Math for Quick Reference

Liquid Volume
1 teaspoon = ⅓ Tablespoon = 4.9mL
3 teaspoons = 1 Tablespoon = 15mL
4 Tablespoons = ¼ cup = 60mL
5 ⅓ Tablespoons = ⅓ cup = 79mL
8 Tablespoons = ½ cup = 118mL
16 Tablespoons = 1 cup = 237mL
1 fluid ounce = 2 Tablespoons = 30mL
8 fluid ounces = 1 cup = 237mL
16 fluid ounces = 2 cups = 1 pint = 473mL
32 fluid ounces = 4 cups = 1 quart = 946mL
128 fluid ounces = 16 cups = 1 gallon = 3.8 liters
1 liter = 2.1 pints = 4.23 cups = 33.8 ounces
1 liter = 1.06 quarts = 0.26 gallons

Dry Weights
0.035 ounces = 1 gram
1 ounce = 28.35 grams
1 pound = 453.59 grams = 0.45 kilograms
2.21 pounds = 1 kilogram

Substitution Options
1 cup plain yogurt + 1 teaspoon lemon juice = 1 cup sour cream
1 cup butter = 1 cup shortening + ½ teaspoon fat
1 cup cake flour = 7/8 cup all-purpose flour
1 egg (in baking) = ¼ cup applesauce
1 egg (in baking) = 1 teaspoon baking soda, 1 Tablespoon vinegar
1 cup milk = 1 cup water + 1 teaspoon butter

Internal Cooking Temperatures

These are the ideal internal temperatures for safe consumption.

Beef
Rare	140° F - 60° C
Medium Rare	150° F - 66° C
Medium	160° F - 70° C
Medium Well	165° F - 74° C
Well Done	170° F - 77° C

Pork
Fresh	185° F - 85° C
Smoked	155° F - 68° C

Chicken/Turkey
Dark Meat	165° F - 74° C
White Meat	160° F - 70° C

Duck/Goose
All Meat	165° F - 74° C

Lamb
Whole Cuts	145° F - 63° C
Ground Lamb	160° F - 70° C

Eggs
Baked Dishes	160° F - 70° C

Fish
Fish with Fins	145° F - 63° C
Shellfish (out of shell)	Until it is white and opaque
Shellfish (in shell)	Until the shells have opened

Leftovers
Reheated	165° F - 74° C

Useful Tips and Tricks

Greasy Soup? Lay a leaf of romaine or iceberg lettuce on the top of the soup pot - it will attract the floating grease and remove much of the fat that's floated to the top.

Soup Too Salty? Cut a potato in half, and drop it into the broth. The potato will help absorb the excess salt. Let it simmer in the broth for about 10 minutes.

Before creaming butter and sugar, rinse your mixing bowl with boiling hot water. They'll cream together faster.

Measuring butter or shortening? Dip a spoon into hot water, and rinse your measuring cup with hot water.

Shredding cheese? Put it in the freezer for 5-10 minutes. Cheese will grate easier, and make less mess.

Cutting cake? Unflavored dental floss cuts a cake cleaner than a knife.

Making pie crust? Keep all of your ingredients VERY cold before you start.

Baking potatoes? After you scrub your potatoes clean, soak them in warm salted water for about 30 minutes before baking.

Juicing citrus? Drop lemons, limes and oranges in a bowl or hot water for about 5 minutes.

Lemon juice has a lot of uses. Sprinkle lemon juice on cut fruit pieces to keep them from browning. Add lemon juice to any roasted vegetables, poultry or fish to elevate the flavor. Scrub pans with scorched bottoms with salt and a half lemon.

Add a splash of milk to simmering potatoes, cauliflower, parsnips and other white vegetables to keep them from darkening too much during cooking.

Most fruit is best, when it feels heavy for its size. If it feels light, or hollow, that's a sign that its old or dried out.

Asparagus should be the size of a pencil or smaller, if you're going to roast or steam them. Larger asparagus can be chopped down for stews, soups or omelettes, but won't be as good to eat on it's own.

Slice boiled eggs with a damp, rinsed knife to keep yolks from crumbling too much.

When boiling eggs, remove from the boiling water then immediately transfer them to a bowl with icewater. The temperature shock will make peeling them FAR easier. Also, use week-old eggs for boiling - the shells come off much easier.

QUICK CUT GUIDE

ROUGH CHOP

Larger pieces, an 1″ or so on each side. Good for long cooking recipes, stews and roasting with meats.

FINE CHOP

Smaller cuts, 1/2″ or so. Better for sauteés and, quicker cooking soups and roasts.

MINCE

Much smaller cuts, 1/4″ or so. Good for quick frying, soups and roasting where you want the vegetables to disappear as much as possible.

Acknowledgments

Endless thanks to: my husband Ryan Sterling for being a willing guinea pig for my gastronomic experimentation; Boe Miller, my frequent partner in crime when it comes to culinary (mis)adventures; Brenda Lee who mocked then forgave my inability to brunoise a carrot; Matt Saretto for being a fearless food nerd with me; Sara Hartman, a culinary provocateur who, as best I can tell, invented cake; Cassidy Dimon, whose fearless palette has been indispensable to my culinary adventure, Brad Hutchinson for always being a "Why Not?" person instead of a "Why?" person; Tristan Uhl, who can create a cocktail from thin air to go with every menu; Maggie Allen who reminds me that being good at lots of different things is okay; and Jeanie Bond and Diane McClure who told me that I knew how to write, and that I should just do it.

And for being willing recipe test subjects over the years, Jennifer Kapolczynski, Rob Sanchez, Joshua Magallanes, Ursula Major, Nick Steiner, Nick Bombacie, Cal Ledbetter, Jona Stultz, and many many more... I thank you.

About the Author

Les Sterling has spent most of his life as a photographer, and visual artist in Chicago, Seattle and Los Angeles. He lives with his husband Ryan and two Bombay cats in Kansas City.

You can see more of his work at www.LesSterling.com
Follow Les on Instagram and Twitter @LesSterling

- Notes -

Lightning Source UK Ltd.
Milton Keynes UK
UKHW050712200223
417303UK00010B/72